C# Database Basics

T0324352

Michael Schmalz

O'REILLY®

Beijing · Cambridge · Farnham · Köln · Sebastopol · Tokyo

C# Database Basics
by Michael Schmalz

Published by O'Reilly Media, Inc., 1005 Gravenstein Highway North, Sebastopol, CA 95472.

O'Reilly books may be purchased for educational, business, or sales promotional use. Online editions are also available for most titles (*http://my.safaribooksonline.com*). For more information, contact our corporate/institutional sales department: (800) 998-9938 or *corporate@oreilly.com*.

Editor: Simon St. Laurent
Production Editor: Holly Bauer
Proofreader: O'Reilly Production Services

Cover Designer: Karen Montgomery
Interior Designer: David Futato
Illustrator: Robert Romano

Revision History for the First Edition:
    2012-01-25   First release
See *http://oreilly.com/catalog/errata.csp?isbn=9781449309985* for release details.

ISBN: 978-1-449-30998-5

[LSI]

1327510162

Table of Contents

Preface

Using databases in C# can be daunting for developers moving from VB6, VBA, or Access. From the differences in the .NET syntax to the curly braces and semicolons, just looking at the code in C# for the first time can be intimidating. As you start to use C#, the small changes you need to make become easier and the code starts to flow nicely. However, you will likely find that many ways of working with data and databases that were easy in VB6 and VBA can be challenging when attempted for the first time in C#.

When you were programming in Classic VB, you could count on a good solid example of how to use a particular method, and it would be in context. For instance, if you were looking at a connection string example, it would likely include how to connect to the database, and it would probably also include a recordset or query. In C# and the other .NET languages, you will find fewer full examples and more examples that simply show the syntax. Or worse, they'll show the other objects in the example, but won't explain how to create those objects or explain where the object needs to be declared (at the form level or at the procedure level).

What led to this book was a challenge that I faced while doing something that I thought should have been very simple. I wanted to create a form with a datagrid that would load a table or query at runtime with the ability to filter, sort, and edit the records. I could do this task with Classic VB in a few minutes and in even less time with VBA inside of Access. With C#, there were pieces that were very simple, but only simple when building the connection to a single database and a single table that you define at design time. Getting code to change the datasource at runtime or connecting to a different table when your database schema changes was significantly more challenging. In addition, the help available online from within Visual Studio or even from an Internet search wasn't very complete. It isn't enough to know the method that you need to call; you need to understand where the variables are declared, the changes that are needed to the properties on the datagrid, the "using" references that are required, etc. Once you see it, the code is very clear, but it is less than straightforward when you are starting out.

Objectives

This book teaches you some specific items to help you get started with C# and databases. You won't tackle a full project, but rather you will get a chance to use C# in a way that helps you learn by example. Many programmers learn best by simply doing: using a concept in code that can eventually be applied to situations in the future. That is the essence of what you will accomplish by reading this book. No knowledge of C# or even VB is really required, but specific differences between Classic VB and C# will be highlighted. You don't even need to purchase any software; you can use the freely available Visual Studio Express and SQL Server Express if you don't have the full version of Visual Studio and/or Microsoft Office (for Access Databases). Also, you should generally be able to cut and paste code that you generate while working through this book to use in your other projects.

When you finish this book, you should be able to do the following:

1. Create a Windows Forms Application with a datagrid
2. Connect to multiple data sources (Access and SQL Server)
3. Add, Edit, and Update database data with a source set at runtime
4. Connect to a datasource at design time that cannot be changed
5. Understand roles of DataTable, DataView, BindingSource, Filters, and other objects
6. Understand that where variables are declared impacts the code
7. Build a simple webservice that connects to a database

As you follow the examples in this book, you will gain confidence in using C# and will be able to leverage this knowledge in other projects. Also, it is worth noting that both VB.Net and C# are powerful languages, and one isn't necessarily better than the other. Typically, in the past, people have used VB and VB.Net for data-rich and line-of-business applications and C# for the enterprise-level applications. But, this distinction is changing. It is true that if you are building a business application, many of the functions that you might want to use, such as net present value or other time value of money calculations, are built in to VB.Net and not to C#, which makes VB.Net the natural choice when you need that functionality. However, given how data-intense the world is becoming, you simply must know how to access, add, update, and delete data in C# if you plan to program with it. You will be able to do that if you follow the examples in this book.

Conventions Used in This Book

The following typographical conventions are used in this book:

Italic
> Indicates new terms, URLs, email addresses, filenames, and file extensions.

`Constant width`
> Used for program listings, as well as within paragraphs to refer to program elements such as variable or function names, databases, data types, environment variables, statements, and keywords.

`Constant width bold`
> Shows commands or other text that should be typed literally by the user.

`Constant width italic`
> Shows text that should be replaced with user-supplied values or by values determined by context.

> This icon signifies a tip, suggestion, or general note.

> This icon indicates a warning or caution.

Using Code Examples

This book is here to help you get your job done. In general, you may use the code in this book in your programs and documentation. You do not need to contact us for permission unless you're reproducing a significant portion of the code. For example, writing a program that uses several chunks of code from this book does not require permission. Selling or distributing a CD-ROM of examples from O'Reilly books does require permission. Answering a question by citing this book and quoting example code does not require permission. Incorporating a significant amount of example code from this book into your product's documentation does require permission.

We appreciate, but do not require, attribution. An attribution usually includes the title, author, publisher, and ISBN. For example: "*C# Database Basics* by Michael Schmalz (O'Reilly). Copyright 2012 Michael Schmalz, 978-1-449-30998-5."

If you feel your use of code examples falls outside fair use or the permission given above, feel free to contact us at *permissions@oreilly.com*.

Safari® Books Online

Safari Books Online is an on-demand digital library that lets you easily search over 7,500 technology and creative reference books and videos to find the answers you need quickly.

With a subscription, you can read any page and watch any video from our library online. Read books on your cell phone and mobile devices. Access new titles before they are available for print, and get exclusive access to manuscripts in development and post feedback for the authors. Copy and paste code samples, organize your favorites, download chapters, bookmark key sections, create notes, print out pages, and benefit from tons of other time-saving features.

O'Reilly Media has uploaded this book to the Safari Books Online service. To have full digital access to this book and others on similar topics from O'Reilly and other publishers, sign up for free at *http://my.safaribooksonline.com*.

How to Contact Us

Please address comments and questions concerning this book to the publisher:

> O'Reilly Media, Inc.
> 1005 Gravenstein Highway North
> Sebastopol, CA 95472
> 800-998-9938 (in the United States or Canada)
> 707-829-0515 (international or local)
> 707-829-0104 (fax)

We have a web page for this book, where we list errata, examples, and any additional information. You can access this page at:

> *http://shop.oreilly.com/product/0636920021469.do*

To comment or ask technical questions about this book, send email to:

> *bookquestions@oreilly.com*

For more information about our books, courses, conferences, and news, see our website at *http://www.oreilly.com*.

Find us on Facebook: *http://facebook.com/oreilly*

Follow us on Twitter: *http://twitter.com/oreillymedia*

Watch us on YouTube: *http://www.youtube.com/oreillymedia*

First Steps: Form with a Datagrid

It's time to dive into C#. Whether you're moving from Visual Basic or Microsoft Access, getting started means moving through a number of things that look familiar but work just a little differently.

Installing Software

If you haven't done it already, you can go to the Microsoft website and download the Express version of Visual Studio 2010 for C#. The site is presently at *http://www.mi crosoft.com/visualstudio/en-us*. At the bottom of the page, you can go to Express Product Downloads, or you can download the 90-day trial of the full version. Links change all the time, so if it isn't there when you look, a simple search from a search engine will direct you to where you can download it. Once you have it installed and opened it, you will see a screen similar to the one shown in Figure 1-1.

If you want the Express version of SQL Server, it is available on the Express Product Downloads page as well. If you don't have Microsoft Access loaded on your computer, you will need this to work with the data examples. The examples we will use are virtually interchangeable between the two platforms. The main difference is the connection string you will use. While SQL Server has many additional features, it is beyond the scope of this book.

Now that you have the programs installed, you are ready to create a new project. To do this, from the main screen in Visual Studio, you can go to File→New Project, or simply press Ctrl+Shift+N to bring up the new project dialog box that you see in Figure 1-2.

If you click on the Windows Forms Application and enter **FirstTestApplication** into the name field in that dialog box, you will get a screen like you see in Figure 1-3. The Solution Explorer will be on the right (if you don't see that, press Ctrl+W, then press

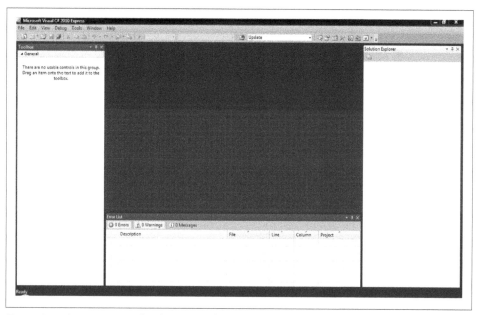

Figure 1-1. The main screen for the Microsoft Visual C# 2010 Express

the S key); it shows all of the objects that are in your solution. (Note that a solution can contain multiple projects.) Below that, you will see the Properties Window, where you will view and edit the object properties. To the left of the screen, you will see the Toolbox Window (you may see more or fewer tools, depending on what you have installed). You can use items in the Toolbox by dragging and dropping onto your form just like you would in Classic VB. At the bottom of the screen, you will notice the Error Window. This window will show you errors and warnings as you write code. This can be very helpful for you as you learn the language. You don't need to wait until you compile to find errors.

Basic Syntax

Most of the work you'll be doing here involves object manipulation, not complex object creation, so you don't need to know the entire C# language to get started. There are some key differences between VB6 and C# that are helpful to be aware of up front. These will be briefly covered here and also in more detail as they come up in the code examples throughout the book.

C# Operators

These can take some time to get used to. The standard Boolean operations that you may have been used to in Classic VB are sometimes the same and sometimes slightly different in C#. In Table 1-1, you will see the VB6 Operator and the C# Operator.

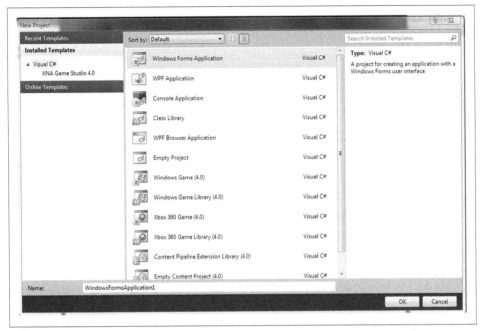

Figure 1-2. The C# New Project Dialog, where you will find the Windows Forms Application

Having compile errors due to using the VB-style operators is easy to fix when you know about it.

Table 1-1. The differences are in the equality and inequality operators. Be careful to use the == when you are testing for equality and = when you are trying to set a value.

Operator Name	VB6 Operator	C# Operator
Equality Operator	=	==
Inequality Operator	<>	!=
Greater Than	>	>
Less Than	<	<
Greater Than or Equal	>=	>=
Less Than or Equal	<=	<=

Outside of the Boolean operators, there are some other slight differences in operators that can save you some time. The first is the increment operator. In VB, you might have done something like:

```
X = X + 1
```

Whereas in C#, you can use:

```
X + = 1;
```

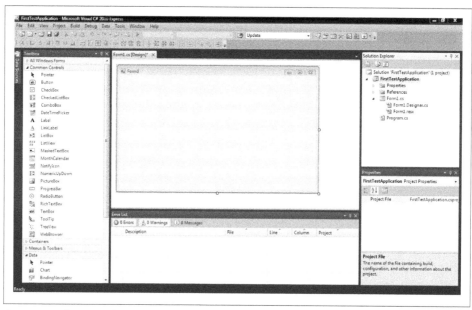

Figure 1-3. The screen for a blank new Windows Forms Application

The addition, subtraction, multiplication, and division increment operators are +=, −=, *=, and /=. So, anywhere that you would use something like X = X (operator) Y, you can use these as shortcuts.

In addition, there are a few other operators that can help you with intense data operations that were not in Classic VB. For example, if you have a situation where you are trying to evaluate an OR expression and each side of the OR expression is data- and processor-intensive, you can use the || operator. Doing this will only evaluate the expressions until it gets a true; once an expression returns true, the statement returns true and the rest of the expressions are not evaluated. In non-processor-intensive operations, you won't get much time savings from this. But, when you are looking at thousands of rows of data for potentially thousands of customers, you might be able to use this operator to save some time. These aren't the only operator changes, however, these are the ones that are relevant to the examples in this book.

Selection Statements

The other changes that can take some getting used to are the selection statements. In Classic VB, we had If ... Then ... Else and Select ... Case. In C#, we have if ... else and switch ... case. Let's assume that we have an integer variable called count that we are trying to evaluate and we have a string variable called reply that we want to populate with a message. See if you can spot the differences compared to VB for both statements:

```
If (count == 0) {
   reply = "The count is 0";
}
else {
 reply = "The count is not 0";
}
switch (count) {
  case 0:
  reply = "The count is 0";
break;
default:
 reply="The count is not 0";
break;
}
```

Notice that in VB, we would have had to use the Then keyword, which is not used in C#. Also, where we would use Select ... Case in VB, we have to use switch ... case. In addition, in VB, we have a capital letter at the beginning of the keywords, whereas in C#, they are in all lowercase. Finally, take note of the braces and semicolons that you don't use in VB. Again, these differences certainly stand out in terms of how they look, but once you write a few statements, you will easily pick up on them.

There are many other differences between the languages—I highlighted these examples because they are often used in data-intensive applications. You can get a full list of operators, keywords, and statements in the help that comes with Visual Studio. Also, the Intellisense in Visual Studio is fantastic and can greatly help you, and the error window also gives surprisingly good help, particularly when you are missing a curly brace, semicolon, or an includes statement.

If you are used to working in Microsoft Access, you can get spoiled by things that are done for you automatically. It is pretty straightforward to make a form in Access that will let you add, update, and delete records. In addition, changing the source data for a grid can really be accomplished with one line of code in VBA. But, building the same functionality from a C# application take some work. Even if you get all of the syntax correct, you have to be careful where you declare objects in C#, where you initialize them, etc. Once you realize where things need to be done, it becomes very easy, and you'll move quickly up the learning curve.

For this example, we will be showing the screens from Visual Studio 2010 Express, but the code doesn't change if you use a different version. In addition, we will be using the Northwind Database that comes with Access. Using the Northwind Database poses some challenges that you will run into when using databases where you don't have control of the schema. These instances will be pointed out and you'll learn how to handle them.

 If you don't have Access or the Northwind Database, you can download the database from the Microsoft website.

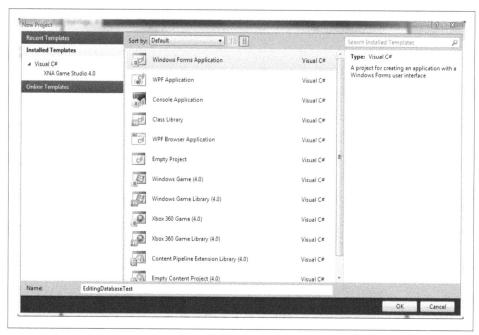

Figure 1-4. The New Project window

First, open up Visual Studio and go to File→New Project. Pick Visual C# and select Windows Forms Application. On the bottom of that dialog box, type in **EditingDatabaseTest** and then click OK, as shown in Figure 1-4. Once you do that, you will see the screen shown in Figure 1-5.

To start with, we'll recreate more or less what Access does automatically when you build a form. You will fill a grid with data, add buttons to filter the data, and have a second grid that will let you choose different tables with which to populate the first grid. In addition, you will be adding code to allow you to add, update, and delete rows of data. While this seems pretty simple, you'll see that there is some planning involved to make this work.

Take a look at the toolbox on the left side of your screen. (If the toolbox isn't there, go to View→Toolbox to show it.) Take notice of the sections—you will be using controls from the Common Controls and Data sections for this sample. On the form, drag on a datagrid from the Data section, a text box from the Common Controls section, a combo box from the Common Controls section, two buttons from the Common Controls section, and a second datagrid from the Data section. When you add the datagrid, you will get the popup dialog shown in Figure 1-6. For the first datagrid, leave the boxes checked to add, update, and delete records. For the second datagrid, uncheck those boxes. On both, leave the datasource as None. You can create a project datasource and use it here, but we are going to start with programming the datasource because it will give you more flexibility. You can lay out these controls however you'd like; you can

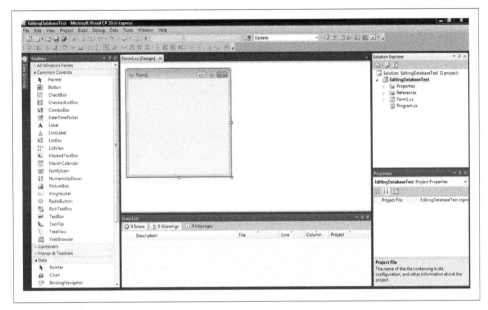

Figure 1-5. Editing your project

Figure 1-6. Choosing data sources for the datagrid

see how I did it in Figure 1-7. If you pressed F5 to start the project, it would open up and nothing would function yet.

Next, you will need to put in some code to get the controls functioning. You can get to the code for a Form by pressing F7, or you can right-click on the form's name in the Solution Explorer on the righthand side of your screen and select View Code from the list. Once there, you will see the lines of code shown in Example 1-1 prefilled for you.

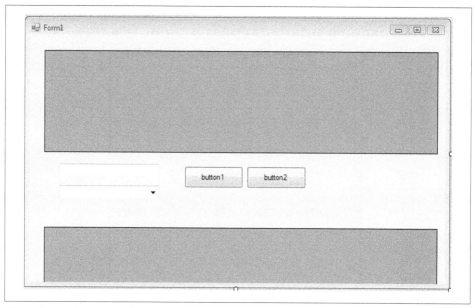

Figure 1-7. An initial form layout

Example 1-1. Basic code to make the controls function

```csharp
using System;
using System.Collections.Generic;
using System.ComponentModel;
using System.Data;
using System.Drawing;
using System.Linq;
using System.Text;
using System.Windows.Forms;

namespace EditingDatabaseTest
{
    public partial class Form1 : Form
    {
        public Form1()
        {
            InitializeComponent();
        }


    }
}
```

The first thing you'll notice in the code is the **using** keyword. These lines of code are very similar to adding a reference in VBA. When you add a **using** directive, it turns on the Intellisense for the objects, properties, and methods related to that namespace.

Please note that you can and often do have to add references to a C# project; I'm only describing it this way to give you a familiar example.

There is an additional using directive that you will need to add for this example to work. Right under using System.Data;, add the following line of code:

```
using System.Data.OleDb;
```

This line of code tells C# to use the .NET Framework Provider for OLE DB. You will use objects, properties, and methods in this namespace to connect to the datasource. Also, you need some of the variables and objects that you are using to remain available continuously while the form is open. For this reason, you need to declare those at the class level and not in the individual procedures that you will be writing. Add the necessary lines to have your code read as shown in Example 1-2.

Example 1-2. Connecting to the datasource with OLE DB

```
using System;
using System.Collections.Generic;
using System.ComponentModel;
using System.Data;
using System.Data.OleDb;
using System.Drawing;
using System.Linq;
using System.Text;
using System.Windows.Forms;

namespace EditingDatabaseTest
{
    public partial class Form1 : Form
    {
        public string connString;
        public string query;
        public OleDbDataAdapter dAdapter;
        public DataTable dTable;
        public OleDbCommandBuilder cBuilder;
        public DataView myDataView;

        public Form1()
        {
            InitializeComponent();
        }


    }
}
```

You need the objects and variables that are declared to remain available because these will be necessary for the updating, sorting, filtering, and other operations that you'll program. If you didn't declare them at the class level, those objects won't be available outside of the procedure in which they were declared. After the Initialize Component(); statement, add the following lines of code:

```
            connString = "Provider=Microsoft.ACE.OLEDB.12.0;Data
    Source=C:\\users\\michael\\documents\\Northwind 2007.accdb";
            query = "SELECT * FROM Customers";
            dAdapter = new OleDbDataAdapter(query, connString);
            dTable = new DataTable();
            cBuilder = new OleDbCommandBuilder(dAdapter);
            cBuilder.QuotePrefix = "[";
            cBuilder.QuoteSuffix = "]";
            myDataView = dTable.DefaultView;
```

The connection string is very similar to what you would see in VBA. However, you should notice the \\ in the path name. If you use a single \, you will get an unrecognized escape sequence error. The query variable is a string that defines the Select statement that you are using to access the data. The OleDbDataAdapter is the class that holds the data commands and connection that you will use to fill the DataTable. The OleDb CommandBuilder class generates the commands that reconcile changes that happen in a DataTable and the connected database.

Since you are connecting to the Northwind Database, you need the QuotePrefix and QuoteSuffix properties defined with the square brackets. This is because the Northwind Database has spaces in the field names. If you try to update a cell in your datagrid that has spaces in field names without these properties defined, you will get an error. You can always trap that error, but it would make updating impossible in tables with spaces in field names. If you don't add these properties and your datasource doesn't have spaces in field names, you will still be able to run error-free. However, I recommend always adding these lines just in case. Next, add the following lines of code to finish up this first procedure:

```
            dAdapter.Fill(dTable);
            BindingSource bndSource = new BindingSource();
            bndSource.DataSource = dTable;
            this.dataGridView1.DataSource = bndSource;
            for (int q = 0; q <= dataGridView1.ColumnCount - 1; q++)
            {
                    this.comboBox1.Items.Add
    (this.dataGridView1.Columns[q].HeaderText.ToString());
            }
            OleDbConnection xyz = new OleDbConnection(connString);
            xyz.Open();
            DataTable tbl = xyz.GetSchema("Tables");

            dataGridView2.DataSource = tbl;
            DataView tbl_dv = tbl.DefaultView;
```

You are accomplishing several things with this code. First, you are filling the Data Table with the data in the data adapter. Then, you are creating a binding source for the form. (The BindingSource class is part of the System.Windows.Forms namespace.) Then, you are finally ready to set the datasource for the datagrid. Once you do this, the data you selected will populate the grid.

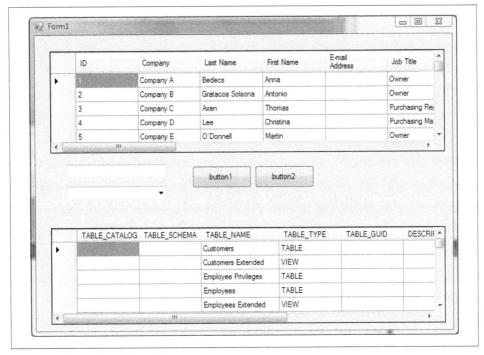

Figure 1-8. A populated datagrid

The next part of the code is a for loop, which is being used to populate the combo box with the field names. The code isn't going to do anything with this data, but you could use that to set the sort field or do any other number of tasks. It is being included here simply to show you an example of how to iterate through the columns of a datagrid.

Finally, the bottom section of that code snippet is being used to populate the second datagrid with the schema of the OleDbConnection.

If you press F5 at this point, the form will open and you will see the screen in Figure 1-8. Because you told the first datagrid that it could add, update, and delete, you will be able to edit those fields. But, you didn't add code yet to reconcile those changes in the database. So, you can edit the field and everything will show on the screen like it is changed; however, if you close the form and open it again, the changes will not be in the database. Also, you will notice that the bottom datagrid cannot be edited. This is because you unchecked the boxes. The important thing to note here is that those settings only impact the grid; they do not impact the database. If you search for help on datagrids in C# online, you will see many questions from people who made the change in the grid but didn't add the code to apply the updates—they can't understand why the data isn't being changed in the database.

So, let's add the code for updates. Add this code right below the curly brace ending the Form1() procedure:

```
private void Cell_Update(object sender, DataGridViewCellEventArgs e)
    {
        try
        {
            dAdapter.Update(dTable);
            this.textBox1.Text = "Updated " + System.DateTime.Now.ToString();
        }
        catch (OleDbException f)
        {
            this.textBox1.Text = "Not Updated " + f.Source.ToString();
        }
    }
```

Once you do this, you need to set up the grid to call this procedure. Switch to the design view screen (Shift+F7), right-click on the first datagrid, and select Properties. On that box, click on the lightning bolt to get to the events and find the event called RowValidated. In that event, select Cell_Update from the drop-down box. It should be the only item available in the list at this time.

When you are creating an application, the last thing you want to do is have your users get dropped to a debug window or throw an unhandled exception. So, what I've done in this section of code is put the code that does the updating in a try ... catch statement. You could accomplish that update in one line of code: dAdapter.Update (dTable);. However, that code can throw an error for any number of reasons. For example, you could be updating a table that doesn't have a primary key defined (that will always throw an error), or you might have skipped the step where you define the QuotePrefix and QuoteSuffix on the command builder and you have a table with spaces in field names. So, when that happens, you want the code to handle that exception gracefully. In this case, the code will try to execute that line and if it works, it will update the text box telling the user that it updated. If there is an OleDbException, it will update the text box, telling the user that it wasn't updated. The grid will also show a red X on the left side of the row that didn't update. Note that you are only trapping an OleDb Exception. You can trap all exceptions instead of defining one, but it is best to write specific sections of code to handle each type of error you may get.

The other item to note is the dAdapter variable. If you declare that variable in the Form1() procedure, it will run fine when the application first starts running, but it will give you an error when writing the update section of code because the dAdapter variable will be out of context.

Adding Filtering

The next thing you are going to program here is the filtering functionality. Go back to the design view on the form and change the button text for the buttons to be Set Filter and Clear Filter. Then come back to the code window and we'll add the procedures for this functionality.

There are a number of ways that you can add filtering functionality. What you'll do here is essentially the filter by selection functionality from Access, but we will default to using the entire field. You can do wildcards and such, but for now, we will focus on the basics. Enter the following code below the update procedure:

```
private void filter_click(object sender, EventArgs e)
    {
        string mystr;
        if (myDataView.RowFilter == "")
        {
            mystr = "[" +
dataGridView1.CurrentCell.OwningColumn.HeaderText.ToString() + "]";
            mystr += " = '" + dataGridView1.CurrentCell.Value.ToString() + "'";
            myDataView.RowFilter = mystr;
        }
        else
        {
            mystr = myDataView.RowFilter + " and ";
            mystr += "[" +
dataGridView1.CurrentCell.OwningColumn.HeaderText.ToString() + "]";
mystr += " = '" + dataGridView1.CurrentCell.Value.ToString() + "'";
            myDataView.RowFilter = mystr;
        }
    }
```

A couple of things are important here. First, there is a line of code checking to see if the grid is already filtered. If the grid is filtered, clicking the filter button again adds to the filter. If the filter is empty, the code just sets the filter. Second, since we are not using the OleDbCommandBuilder class here, the brackets will not be added to our column names automatically. So, you just need to add the square bracket to the front and back of the column name. Finally, you should take a look at all of the properties and methods that are available on the CurrentCell. In this case, you are referencing the OwningColumn of the cell and the HeaderText of that column; the HeaderText is the same as the field name in the table. Also, as in the other procedure, the object that we are referring to (myDataView in this case) is declared at the class level, so it is available to all procedures in the form.

Next, you will want to set this code to run when the Set Filter button is clicked. So, go back to the design view and right-click on the first button (you should have already set the Text property to Set Filter), then click on the lightning bolt to show the events. Find the click event and in the drop-down box, select filter_click.

Go back to the code view and add the following lines of code underneath the filter_click procedure:

```
private void clear_filter(object sender, EventArgs e)
    {
        myDataView.RowFilter = "";
    }
```

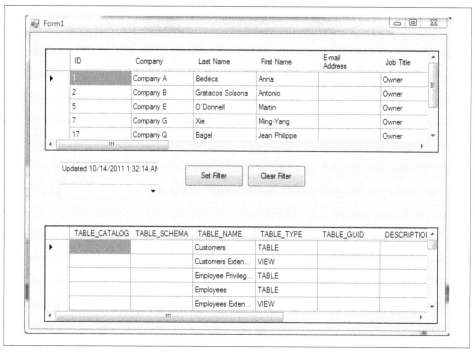

Figure 1-9. Setting a filter

Switch back to the design view and set the click event for the second button to clear_filter, just like you did for the first button. You may notice that only clear_ filter and filter_click are available when you have another event already programmed for the row updating. This is because the Cell_Update procedure is specific to DataGridViewCellEventArgs, so it will only show up for datagrid events.

Once you have done this, press F5, and when the form opens, click in the first cell under Job Title, which should say owner. Then click on the button to Set Filter. You will see a form like the one shown in Figure 1-9.

If you click Clear Filter, it will remove the Filter. This functionality is fairly simple, but you can see how actually programming it is a bit complex. It wouldn't make sense to go through all of this if all we wanted to do was edit a static table. If you wanted to do that, you could create a project datasource, which would set the code to allow updates, adds, deletes, etc. So, what I'm trying to show here is how you can select a different table and populate the first datagrid.

Your next task is to add another button to the form and call it Change Source. Add the following code below the last procedure you wrote:

```
private void change_data_source(object sender, EventArgs e)
    {
        string tbl_str = dataGridView2.CurrentRow.Cells[2].Value.ToString();
        query = "SELECT * FROM [" + tbl_str + "]";
```

```
            dAdapter = new OleDbDataAdapter(query, connString);
            dTable = new DataTable();
            cBuilder = new OleDbCommandBuilder(dAdapter);
            cBuilder.QuotePrefix = "[";
            cBuilder.QuoteSuffix = "]";
            myDataView = dTable.DefaultView;
            dAdapter.Fill(dTable);
            BindingSource bSource = new BindingSource();
            bSource.DataSource = dTable;
            this.dataGridView1.DataSource = bSource;

            for (int q = 0; q <= dataGridView1.ColumnCount - 1; q++)
            {
    this.comboBox1.Items.Add(this.dataGridView1.Columns[q].HeaderText.ToString());
            }

        }
```

This is essentially the same code as our opening code except that we are setting the table name equal to the third column of the schema grid. Please note that the columns of the grid are 0-based, so the third column has an int index of 2. Once you've done this, go back to the design view and set the click event to change_data_source. Your final form should look like the one shown in Figure 1-10.

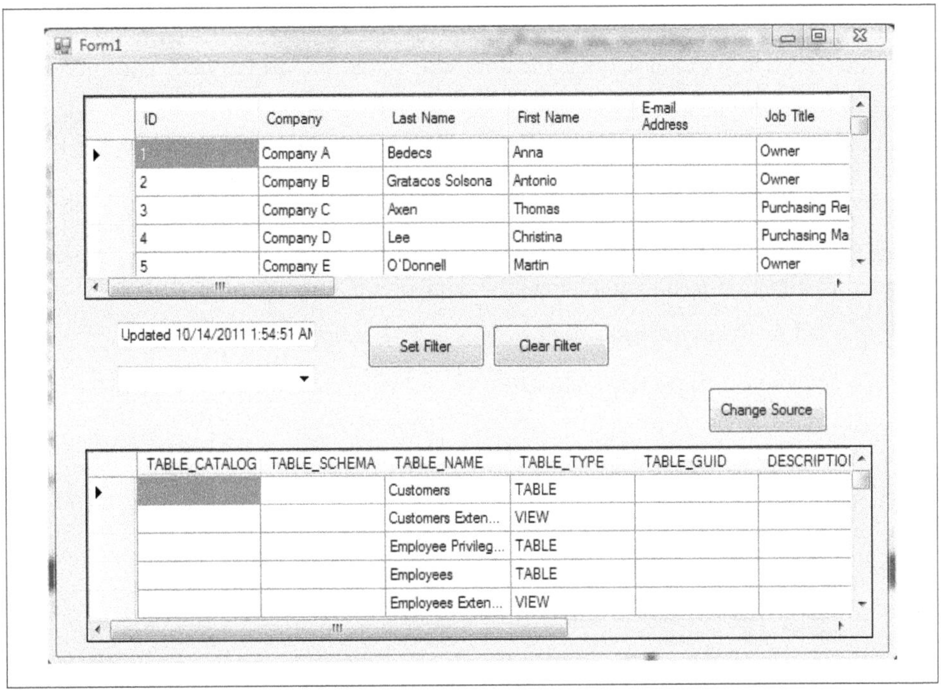

Figure 1-10. Form with an added Change Source button

Some Other Considerations

You should be aware of some errors that you will see with the datagrid, particularly with the Northwind Database. If you try to add records to some tables, you will see a red exclamation point to the left of the row, and if you hover over it, you will see "An INSERT INTO query cannot contain a multi-valued field." This is because some of the tables in the Northwind Database take advantage of an Access-only feature of storing more than one value in a field (for example, multiple examples from a list). Since you won't be able to insert records into the database if your table has a field like that, I would avoid it if you are planning on updating outside of Access.

Let's take a look at a situation where you can update. In the second datagrid, click on the cell that says Invoices (you will need to scroll down), and then click the Change Source button. The data in the first datagrid will change to show the Invoices table. Then scroll down to the bottom and try to add a new row. Use 125 as the Order ID and use 7/1/2011 as the Invoice Date, then put zeroes in the columns with numbers. Then tab down to the next row or click off the row that you are trying to add.

When you do this, you will get a red exclamation point. When you hover over it, it will tell you that you need a related record in the table Orders. So, change the Order ID to 58 (which exists in the Orders table), and then click off the row. You will see that the update works. Then, click on Inventory Transactions (right above Invoices in the bottom grid) and click on Change Source. Then, go right back to Invoices and hit the Change Source button again. If you scroll to the bottom, you will see the row of data that you added and you'll see that the database added the primary key automatically.

Now, you can try to delete that row. Click on the space right to the left of the first column on that row that you added. This will highlight the row. Now press the Delete key. This deletes the row from the database.

You can see from this example that while this is slightly more complicated than doing the same thing in Access, once you have the pattern down, it is relatively straightforward to add a datagrid and change the datasource, filter, etc.

Example 1-3 provides the full code listing for the example in this chapter.

Example 1-3. Putting all of the code together

```
using System;
using System.Collections.Generic;
using System.ComponentModel;
using System.Data;
using System.Data.OleDb;
using System.Drawing;
using System.Linq;
using System.Text;
using System.Windows.Forms;

namespace EditingDatabaseTest
{
```

```csharp
    public partial class Form1 : Form
    {
        public string connString;
        public string query;
        public OleDbDataAdapter dAdapter;
        public DataTable dTable;
        public OleDbCommandBuilder cBuilder;
        public DataView myDataView;

        public Form1()
        {
            InitializeComponent();
            connString = "Provider=Microsoft.ACE.OLEDB.12.0;
Data Source=C:\\users\\michael\\documents\\Northwind 2007.accdb";
            query = "SELECT * FROM Customers";
            dAdapter = new OleDbDataAdapter(query, connString);
            dTable = new DataTable();
            cBuilder = new OleDbCommandBuilder(dAdapter);
            cBuilder.QuotePrefix = "[";
            cBuilder.QuoteSuffix = "]";
            myDataView = dTable.DefaultView;
            dAdapter.Fill(dTable);
            BindingSource bndSource = new BindingSource();
            bndSource.DataSource = dTable;
            this.dataGridView1.DataSource = bndSource;
            for (int q = 0; q <= dataGridView1.ColumnCount - 1; q++)
            {
this.comboBox1.Items.Add(this.dataGridView1.Columns[q].HeaderText.ToString());
            }
            OleDbConnection xyz = new OleDbConnection(connString);
            xyz.Open();
            DataTable tbl = xyz.GetSchema("Tables");

            dataGridView2.DataSource = tbl;
            DataView tbl_dv = tbl.DefaultView;
        }

        private void Cell_Update(object sender, DataGridViewCellEventArgs e)
        {
            try
            {
                dAdapter.Update(dTable);
                this.textBox1.Text = "Updated " + System.DateTime.Now.ToString();
            }
            catch (OleDbException f)
            {
                this.textBox1.Text = "Not Updated " + f.Source.ToString();
            }
        }

        private void filter_click(object sender, EventArgs e)
        {
            string mystr;
            if (myDataView.RowFilter == "")
```

```csharp
            {
                mystr = "[" + dataGridView1.CurrentCell.OwningColumn.HeaderText.ToString()
+ "]";
                mystr += " = '" + dataGridView1.CurrentCell.Value.ToString() + "'";
                myDataView.RowFilter = mystr;
            }
            else
            {
                mystr = myDataView.RowFilter + " and ";
                mystr += "[" + dataGridView1.CurrentCell.OwningColumn.HeaderText.ToString()
+ "]";
                mystr += " = '" + dataGridView1.CurrentCell.Value.ToString() + "'";
                myDataView.RowFilter = mystr;
            }
        }

        private void clear_filter(object sender, EventArgs e)
        {
            myDataView.RowFilter = "";
        }

        private void change_data_source(object sender, EventArgs e)
        {
            string tbl_str = dataGridView2.CurrentRow.Cells[2].Value.ToString();
            query = "SELECT * FROM [" + tbl_str + "]";
            dAdapter = new OleDbDataAdapter(query, connString);
            dTable = new DataTable();
            cBuilder = new OleDbCommandBuilder(dAdapter);
            cBuilder.QuotePrefix = "[";
            cBuilder.QuoteSuffix = "]";
            myDataView = dTable.DefaultView;
            dAdapter.Fill(dTable);
            BindingSource bSource = new BindingSource();
            bSource.DataSource = dTable;
            this.dataGridView1.DataSource = bSource;

            for (int q = 0; q <= dataGridView1.ColumnCount - 1; q++)
            {
this.comboBox1.Items.Add(this.dataGridView1.Columns[q].HeaderText.ToString());
            }

        }


    }
}
```

Before we head to the next chapter and connect to SQL Server, let's review some of the differences between data access inside of Microsoft Access and from C#. One of the biggest challenges is setting the events to fire at the right time and declaring the variables in the right place. In this example, it was done for you. But when you are writing from scratch, it is easy to get this part wrong. You'll know when it happens when you try to access a variable that Visual Studio says is out of context. So, when that happens, you'll know exactly where to look.

The events are a little trickier. As an example, some people will go through the events that are available in the datagrid, and they might choose an event like `CellEndEdit` to put the update code in. However, you will end up with errors when you try to add new rows because you will be missing required fields when the update fires right after the first column is updated. If you look around some of the technology forums, you'll see some debate about where to fire the update event. My personal opinion is that doing it after the row validates is best, as it will only fire when you leave a row. You also have the option of having a Save button and only firing the updates when that button is pressed. The point is that you have options for when you call events and you can test them to see where it works the best in your particular application.

The final item of importance is to understand when you are dealing with an object or control that is in the Windows Forms namespace or the `System.Data` namespace, and when you are in the `System.Data.OleDb` namespace. There are times when you may want to try something, but you can't find the object or method that you want. When you run into situations like that, all you need to do is hover over the class name where you declare the variable and it will tell you what namespace that class is in.

What's Next?

The next chapter will connect SQL Server. If you don't have SQL Server, you can download SQL Server Express. In addition, you will see some other examples in future chapters on databinding without a grid and even on returning data from a database on a webservice. This first coding chapter really lays the foundation for everything else that is covered. If you want to take advantage of what's next, you will want to make sure you understand everything in this chapter before you move on.

CHAPTER 2

C# Data Access to SQL Server

While building an Access database is usually enough to get data access for your application, you are often trying to get at data that already exists. Many times, that data exists in SQL Server or another ODBC database. So, the examples in this chapter will use data that exists in the sample databases provided by Microsoft. When using SQL Server 2008, the sample databases are not installed by default. You can download Northwind or Pubs and install them, but in this chapter, I will be basing the examples on the AdventureWorks database that is available on the Microsoft website.

The nice thing about accessing the data with SQL Server as the backend database is that almost all of your code will still work. So, if you have data in Microsoft Access and you move it to SQL Server, you don't need to go back to the drawing board on every line of code. Certainly, you will have to make some changes, but you can get Visual Studio to identify them for you.

In this chapter, you'll take the example from Chapter 2 and make the minimum changes to get the data to work with SQL Server. First, I will cover what needs to be changed and then I will show you a shortcut. To get started, take your directory from the last chapter, which should have been called EditingDatabaseTest, make a copy of it, and paste it into the same folder. When you do this, change the name from EditingDatabaseTest – Copy to **EditingDatabaseTest_SQL**. You don't need to change the project solution file name. (You certainly could, but I didn't do that here.)

Open up that project and go into the code for Form1 (you can right-click on Form1 in the Solution Explorer and click View Code) and you will see the code that you wrote in the previous chapter. In the last chapter, we used the following line of code to tell Visual Studio that we wanted to use the OleDB provider:

```
using System.Data.OleDb;
```

While you can connect to multiple data sources with the OleDB provider, C# has a special type for SQL Server, which is what you want to use when you are working with SQL Server. To do that, you just need to change that line to:

```
using System.Data.SqlClient;
```

Figure 2-1. Trying to make a change simply produces errors

When you do that (provided that you change the existing line and don't simply write a new line), you will see nine errors come up in the error list, as shown in Figure 2-1.

The errors are caused by the change from `System.Data.OleDb` to `System.Data.Sql Client`. All of the objects that are in `System.Data.OleDb` are no longer available to be used because that reference is gone. While that might sound bad, it actually makes it very easy for you to find what to change.

Before you go to fix any errors, you need to make sure that your SQL Server is running and that you are using Integrated Security (meaning it is going to use your Windows User Account to access the database) on the Adventure Works database (if you didn't install that database yet, you should do that now). There are six Adventure Works databases that install with the download from Microsoft. What you will be using is just the AdventureWorks database, however, this code will work with really any other SQL Server database.

Once you have verified that your server is running, you will need to change the connection string that you have from the Access database to your SQL Server database. The following code:

```
connString = "Provider=Microsoft.ACE.OLEDB.12.0;Data Source=C:\\users\\michael\
\documents\\Northwind 2007.accdb";
```

becomes:

```
connString = "Data Source=.\\Server_Name;Initial Catalog=AdventureWorks;Integrated
Security=True;";
```

For Server_Name, you need to enter the name of your SQL Server Database. In SQL Server Management Studio, it is in the first line in the Object Explorer. It will have your computer name\server name. In this case, I am showing an example of connecting to a server on the same machine, so I use .\\Server_Name because the "." refers to the local machine, but it could be replaced with something else like: IP Address\Server_Name or Computer_Name\Server_Name. If you run into any issues finding out how you connect to a remote machine (for example, a SQL Server database on a web server), generally the administrator can get you the connection string. Later in this book, connecting to SQL Server with a username and password is also covered.

The only thing the connection string is doing for you is telling it where the SQL Server is, what database you should connect to (Initial Catalog), and that you are using the Windows User's permissions to log in to the database.

You may have noticed that in the SQL Server Object Browser, there is a single \ in between the computer and server names, but in the line of code, there are two \'s. The reason for that is that a single \ in regular quotes is taken as an escape sequence. It will tell you that it is an unrecognized escape sequence. So, you fix it by putting in two \'s, or you can change the line to:

```
connString = @"Data Source=.\MJS_SQL;Initial Catalog=AdventureWorks;Integrated
Security=True;";
```

Either way will work—I generally put in the double forward slashes, but it doesn't matter which one you use. The next thing you need to change is the initial query because the table structure is different. I made the query string:

```
query = "SELECT * FROM HumanResources.Employee";
```

You could pick any table in that database; I just chose this one randomly. One of the changes that you'll notice in SQL Server is that there is a Table_Schema and a Table_Name. In a lot of cases, you will see dbo as the Table_Schema, but in the AdventureWorks database, they use dbo, HumanResources, Person, Production, Purchasing, and Sales. Since you don't always know ahead of time if you are going to need it, you should always include both in your code.

Now that you have done that, the only other changes that need to be made are with the object types. Here are the lines that should show errors for you:

```
public OleDbDataAdapter dAdapter;
public OleDbCommandBuilder cBuilder;
dAdapter = new OleDbDataAdapter(query, connString);
cBuilder = new OleDbCommandBuilder(dAdapter);
OleDbConnection xyz = new OleDbConnection(connString);
catch (OleDbException f)
dAdapter = new OleDbDataAdapter(query, connString);
cBuilder = new OleDbCommandBuilder(dAdapter);
```

You should notice that all of the error object types have OleDb as the prefix. You can edit each of these to the Sql prefixed object. Or, you can do a simple Find .. Replace and do a search for OleDb and set the replace to be Sql (case is important on both).

You should get nine replacements (eight lines of code with one line having the object type twice).

If you run this program, it will work until you try to change the table name using the Change Source button. This is because you need the schema name. This is a very easy fix. The lines that read:

```
string tbl_str = dataGridView2.CurrentRow.Cells[2].Value.ToString();
query = "SELECT * FROM [" + tbl_str + "]";
```

become:

```
        string tbl_str = "[" + dataGridView2.CurrentRow.Cells[1].Value.ToString()
  + "].[" + dataGridView2.CurrentRow.Cells[2].Value.ToString() + "]";
        query = "SELECT * FROM " + tbl_str + "";
```

This looks complicated but is very straightforward. Since you can't be sure of the Schema or Field Names, you need to put brackets around them. (Remember that you already have lines of code that designate the brackets to be used by setting the Quote Prefix and QuoteSuffix, but that only applies to the SqlCommandBuilder object, meaning that when it builds the commands for the Create, Read, Update, and Delete operations, it will automatically include the brackets, but not in normal queries.) Since the columns are a zero-based collection, you refer to Cell 1 and Cell 2 for columns 2 and 3. See Figure 2-2 for the difference in the database table information. We have four columns of data in the SQL Client's table information compared to the nine columns in the OleDB provider's.

If you run the code, you will see that you can edit rows, add rows, etc. The only changes that you needed to make were to the connection string and object types, and then you needed to add the Schema Name to the table that you selected when you clicked the Change Source button. All of the filtering of data, filling of the grid, etc., is exactly the same as it is with the OleDb datasource.

There are some other things that you can use here as well as in the OleDb objects. For example, if the data you wanted was in a view instead of in a table, you would just change one line of code:

```
DataTable tbl = xyz.GetSchema("Tables");
```

becomes

```
DataTable tbl = xyz.GetSchema("Views");
```

When you do this and open it up, you will see something like Figure 2-3.

When you look at this, you should notice that the IS_UPDATABLE flag is set to NO for all of the views. So, everything will seem great until you try to update a row. If you change the source to vEmployee and try to change data in a cell, you will get an error on this line:

```
dAdapter.Update(dTable);
```

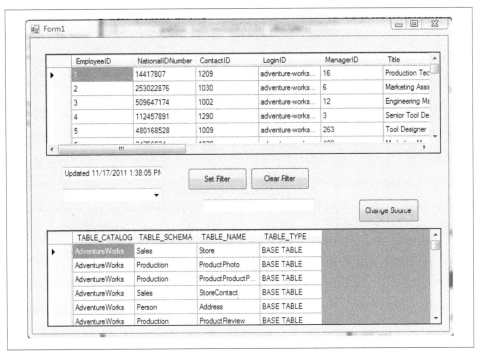

Figure 2-2. Different database information

This is because the error we were trapping on Cell Update was a `SqlException`. However, a table that cannot be updated is an `InvalidOperationException`. There are couple of things you can do here. You can make the code that reads:

```
catch (SqlException  f)
```

become:

```
catch (Exception  f)
```

That is fine, but it will catch every type of exception. So, let's assume that you want to do something different for an invalid operation. For now, you will set it to tell you in a message box and to update the box to tell you that it wasn't updated. If you don't know what type of exception that error is, you can run it to get the error and the box will tell you what type of exception was unhandled. See the box in Figure 2-4.

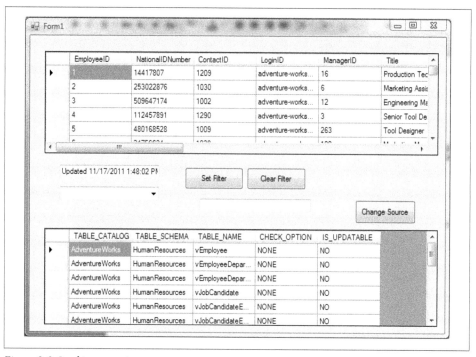

Figure 2-3. Looking at a view

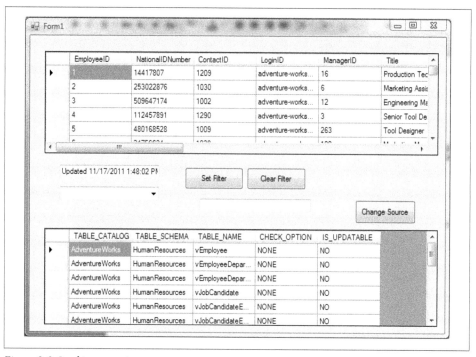

Figure 2-4. Error reporting

You can just enter in the code for the InvalidOperationException inside the current try ... catch statement. It will look like this:

```
private void Cell_Update(object sender, DataGridViewCellEventArgs e)
    {
        try
        {
            dAdapter.Update(dTable);
            this.textBox1.Text = "Updated " + System.DateTime.Now.ToString();
        }
        catch (InvalidOperationException f)
            {
                MessageBox.Show("Operation is not allowed");
                this.textBox1.Text = "Not Updated " + f.Source.ToString();
            }
        catch (SqlException  f)
        {
            this.textBox1.Text = "Not Updated " + f.Source.ToString();
        }
    }
```

While this is a simple example, in a real-world situation, you could have certain exceptions send emails to a particular team of people and have another write data to a log file, etc. The key is that during your testing, you should try to figure out errors that your users could have, then you can trap them in the try ... catch loops. There are a lot of times that I just don't know what type of errors I could even get, and letting the error happen lets me trap each one differently. Again, you can just catch all with Exception, but you might be sweeping a away a problem that you would want to know about. So, my recommendation is to trap each one separately versus having a catchall.

There are clearly many other things that you might want to do with SQL Server, and there are some additional examples in the book. The key items are covered here, and if you want to populate a grid and let people do editing on a desktop application, this simple application gets it done.

The full code listing follows:

```
using System;
using System.Collections.Generic;
using System.ComponentModel;
using System.Data;
using System.Data.SqlClient;
using System.Drawing;
using System.Linq;
using System.Text;
using System.Windows.Forms;

namespace EditingDatabaseTest
{
    public partial class Form1 : Form
    {
        public string connString;
        public string query;
        public SqlDataAdapter dAdapter;
```

```
            public DataTable dTable;
            public SqlCommandBuilder cBuilder;
            public DataView myDataView;

            public Form1()
            {
                InitializeComponent();
                connString = "Data Source=.\\MJS_SQL;Initial
Catalog=AdventureWorks;Integrated Security=True;";
                query = "SELECT * FROM HumanResources.Employee";
                dAdapter = new SqlDataAdapter(query, connString);
                dTable = new DataTable();
                cBuilder = new SqlCommandBuilder(dAdapter);
                cBuilder.QuotePrefix = "[";
                cBuilder.QuoteSuffix = "]";
                myDataView = dTable.DefaultView;
                dAdapter.Fill(dTable);
                BindingSource bndSource = new BindingSource();
                bndSource.DataSource = dTable;
                this.dataGridView1.DataSource = bndSource;
                for (int q = 0; q <= dataGridView1.ColumnCount - 1; q++)
                {

this.comboBox1.Items.Add(this.dataGridView1.Columns[q].HeaderText.ToString());
                }
                SqlConnection xyz = new SqlConnection(connString);
                xyz.Open();
                DataTable tbl = xyz.GetSchema("Tables");

                dataGridView2.DataSource = tbl;
                DataView tbl_dv = tbl.DefaultView;
            }

            private void Cell_Update(object sender, DataGridViewCellEventArgs e)
            {
                try
                {
                    dAdapter.Update(dTable);
                    this.textBox1.Text = "Updated " + System.DateTime.Now.ToString();
                }
                catch (InvalidOperationException f)
                    {
                        MessageBox.Show("Operation is not allowed");
                        this.textBox1.Text = "Not Updated " + f.Source.ToString();
                    }
                catch (SqlException  f)
                {
                    this.textBox1.Text = "Not Updated " + f.Source.ToString();
                }
            }

            private void filter_click(object sender, EventArgs e)
            {
                string mystr;
                if (myDataView.RowFilter == "")
```

```
        {
            mystr = "[" +
dataGridView1.CurrentCell.OwningColumn.HeaderText.ToString() + "]";
            mystr += " = '" + dataGridView1.CurrentCell.Value.ToString() + "'";
            myDataView.RowFilter = mystr;
        }
        else
        {
            mystr = myDataView.RowFilter + " and ";
            mystr += "[" +
dataGridView1.CurrentCell.OwningColumn.HeaderText.ToString() + "]";
            mystr += " = '" + dataGridView1.CurrentCell.Value.ToString() + "'";
            myDataView.RowFilter = mystr;
        }
    }

    private void clear_filter(object sender, EventArgs e)
    {
        myDataView.RowFilter = "";
    }

    private void change_data_source(object sender, EventArgs e)
    {
        string tbl_str = "[" + dataGridView2.CurrentRow.Cells[1].Value.ToString()
+ "].[" + dataGridView2.CurrentRow.Cells[2].Value.ToString() + "]";
        query = "SELECT * FROM " + tbl_str + "";
        dAdapter = new SqlDataAdapter(query, connString);
        dTable = new DataTable();
        cBuilder = new SqlCommandBuilder(dAdapter);
        cBuilder.QuotePrefix = "[";
        cBuilder.QuoteSuffix = "]";
        myDataView = dTable.DefaultView;
        dAdapter.Fill(dTable);
        BindingSource bSource = new BindingSource();
        bSource.DataSource = dTable;
        this.dataGridView1.DataSource = bSource;

        for (int q = 0; q <= dataGridView1.ColumnCount - 1; q++)
        {
this.comboBox1.Items.Add(this.dataGridView1.Columns[q].HeaderText.ToString());
        }

    }


  }
}
```

What's Next

Chapter 3 shows how to make a data entry form that isn't on a grid like you would see in a typical Access database application. What is very straightforward in Microsoft Access becomes challenging to implement in C#. You'll also learn how easy it is to deal with related records in multiple tables in a DataSet. If you think about how you have multiple forms (Parent/Child) in an Access application, you can do something very similar in C#, but you can do it within a single form. While there is some complexity that initially seems difficult, I think you'll find the flexibility that you gain is worth the effort.

CHAPTER 3

Building Data Entry Forms

Building data entry forms has always been pretty simple in Access VBA and even Classic VB. This process is more complicated in C#, and really any of the .NET languages. When using DAO and ADO, the main data object is the recordset, which is connected to the database, and you can easily move through records and perform all of the CRUD operations (create, read, update, and delete). You can certainly do all of those things in C#, but the data objects that you will be working with are disconnected, which means that you will need to take explicit steps to keep the datasource in sync with the changes.

There are controls in Visual Studio that can help you build a data entry form and navigate through the records. Those controls won't be covered until the next chapter. While it is less likely that you'll need to make a data entry form that dynamically adjusts to different datasources, it is still useful to build the data connections with code, even if it is just to help you understand what is happening behind the scenes when you use the controls.

The first thing that will be covered is a simple change to the project that we covered in Chapter 2. What you'll be doing is adding a couple buttons to the form to allow you to browse through the records. Also, you will be adding a text box that will bind to a field in the table, and you will be able to make edits to the table in the grid or in the text box. This is an unlikely scenario in the real world, but it is a good learning exercise for how to build a data entry form that will work with multiple tables.

Once you have done this, you will be building a simple data entry form for a specific table. Again, you might find it easier to use the controls provided in Visual Studio in the future, but going through this exercise will be helpful for future programming.

Also, before explaining these items, there are a couple of things that you should know about the .NET objects that we have been and will be using. In the example in Chapter 2, we used a DataTable to get the data. There is another object called a DataSet, which contains a collection of the DataTables that you are connecting to. The Data Set contains information about the relationships between tables in the DataSet. This lets you navigate through parent records and also show the child records at the same time. If you think about a form/sub-form in Access, this is the way that you can achieve similar functionality in C#. However, you don't need to create a separate form to browse and edit the child records; you will be doing everything in one form. You will find that it is very convenient to have all the data you are working with in one object. Also, the same objects that you are going to be creating are created when you use the built-in controls.

Binding a TextBox to Data

When you are binding data, you will need the `BindingSource` object available while the form is open, and you will also need a couple extra controls on the form. So, for this example, you just need to put a label (named `label1`), a text box (named `textbox3`), and a button (named `button4`) on the form. It really doesn't matter where you put them for this example, but in the screenshot, you will see that I put them at the bottom of the form. To make the `BindingSource` object available, you need to put the following line of code up where you are defining variables at the class level:

```
public BindingSource bndSource;
```

Then you will need to add the following lines of code at the bottom of the `Form1()` and `change_data_source` procedures:

```
this.textBox3.DataBindings.Add(new Binding("Text", bndSource,
this.dataGridView1.Columns[1].HeaderText.ToString(),true));
this.label1.Text = this.dataGridView1.Columns[1].HeaderText.ToString();
```

The first line is setting the `DataBindings` property of the textbox control. That property is a collection of data bindings for the control. You can link any number of properties for the control to data. In this case, the property of the control that we want to drive is the `Text` property—this is what drives the display on the screen. Going from left to right, you are adding a binding to the collection, then creating a new binding object. The new binding object takes the following parameters: property name, data source, data member, and a formatting flag. Since for this hypothetical example we don't know the name of the field that we are binding to, we are just using the name of the second column (the column numbers are zero-based, so `Columns[1]` is the second column). The example uses the second column because I didn't want to link to the primary key, in order to show how we can update data. The last line of code sets the text for the label to be the name of the field that you are binding to.

The last step is to set a click event for the button to move through the data. You could add multiple buttons, but this is really just to demonstrate this concept, so one button is fine for now. There is only one line of code needed within the event to do this:

```
private void button4_Click(object sender, EventArgs e)
    {
        bndSource.MoveNext();
    }
```

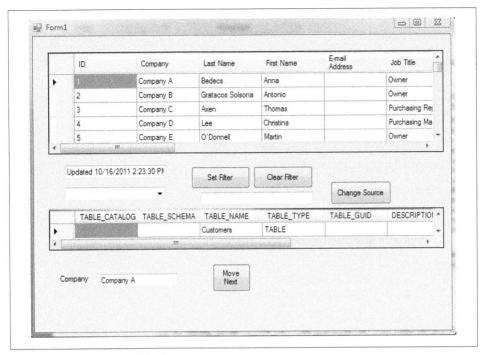

Figure 3-1. Current state of the form

We are missing one line of code, but I want you to run this to see where the error is. When you open this, you will see the screen shown in Figure 3-1.

You can click the Move Next button and you will see that your text box updates with the Company field. You will also see that the current record in the datagrid is moving as well. This is because the binding object is being shared by both. So, where is the error? Well, if you pick a different table and click the Change Source button, you will see an error on the line where you are setting the bindings. This is because there is already a binding to the Text property. So, you will need to add the following line of code above the line where you are setting the binding in the change_data_source procedure:

```
this.textBox3.DataBindings.Clear();
```

All this line of code does is remove all the bindings for that control. If you run it again, you will be able to change tables without error. Because we are still using the datagrid, we already have code that is updating the datasource (it is on the RowValidated event). So, you will be able to edit data in the text box or up in the grid, and when you move around with the button or within the datagrid, you will see that the data updates on the screen and in the database. You will see later that we need to add code to accomplish the edits when we aren't using the datagrid, and it is really unlikely that you would have both a datagrid and a text box like we have here. However, this demonstrates how to use the bindings to get a control to sync up with data in the database.

The full code combining all these changes is shown below:

```
using System;
using System.Collections.Generic;
using System.ComponentModel;
using System.Data;
using System.Data.OleDb;
using System.Drawing;
using System.Linq;
using System.Text;
using System.Windows.Forms;

namespace EditingDatabaseTest
{
    public partial class Form1 : Form
    {
        public string connString;
        public string query;
        public OleDbDataAdapter dAdapter;
        public DataTable dTable;
        public OleDbCommandBuilder cBuilder;
        public DataView myDataView;
        public BindingSource bndSource;

        public Form1()
        {
            InitializeComponent();
            connString = "Provider=Microsoft.ACE.OLEDB.12.0;Data Source=C:\\users\
\michael\\documents\\Northwind 2007.accdb";
            query = "SELECT * FROM Customers";
            dAdapter = new OleDbDataAdapter(query, connString);
            dTable = new DataTable();
            cBuilder = new OleDbCommandBuilder(dAdapter);
            cBuilder.QuotePrefix = "[";
            cBuilder.QuoteSuffix = "]";
            myDataView = dTable.DefaultView;
            dAdapter.Fill(dTable);
            bndSource = new BindingSource();
            bndSource.DataSource = dTable;
            this.dataGridView1.DataSource = bndSource;
            for (int q = 0; q <= dataGridView1.ColumnCount - 1; q++)
            {

this.comboBox1.Items.Add(this.dataGridView1.Columns[q].HeaderText.ToString());
            }
            OleDbConnection xyz = new OleDbConnection(connString);
            xyz.Open();
            DataTable tbl = xyz.GetSchema("Tables");

            dataGridView2.DataSource = tbl;
            DataView tbl_dv = tbl.DefaultView;

            this.textBox3.DataBindings.Add(new Binding("Text", bndSource,
                this.dataGridView1.Columns[1].HeaderText.ToString(),true));
            this.label1.Text = this.dataGridView1.Columns[1].HeaderText.ToString();
        }
```

```csharp
        private void Cell_Update(object sender, DataGridViewCellEventArgs e)
        {
            try
            {
                dAdapter.Update(dTable);
                this.textBox1.Text = "Updated " + System.DateTime.Now.ToString();
            }
            catch (OleDbException f)
            {
                this.textBox1.Text = "Not Updated " + f.Source.ToString();
            }
        }

        private void filter_click(object sender, EventArgs e)
        {
            string mystr;
            if (myDataView.RowFilter == "")
            {
                mystr = "[" +
dataGridView1.CurrentCell.OwningColumn.HeaderText.ToString() + "]";
                mystr += " = '" + dataGridView1.CurrentCell.Value.ToString() + "'";
                myDataView.RowFilter = mystr;
            }
            else
            {
                mystr = myDataView.RowFilter + " and ";
                mystr += "[" +
dataGridView1.CurrentCell.OwningColumn.HeaderText.ToString() + "]";
                mystr += " = '" + dataGridView1.CurrentCell.Value.ToString() + "'";
                myDataView.RowFilter = mystr;
            }
        }

        private void clear_filter(object sender, EventArgs e)
        {
            myDataView.RowFilter = "";
        }

        private void change_data_source(object sender, EventArgs e)
        {
            string tbl_str = dataGridView2.CurrentRow.Cells[2].Value.ToString();
            query = "SELECT * FROM [" + tbl_str + "]";
            dAdapter = new OleDbDataAdapter(query, connString);
            dTable = new DataTable();
            cBuilder = new OleDbCommandBuilder(dAdapter);
            cBuilder.QuotePrefix = "[";
            cBuilder.QuoteSuffix = "]";
            myDataView = dTable.DefaultView;
            dAdapter.Fill(dTable);
            bndSource = new BindingSource();
            bndSource.DataSource = dTable;
            this.dataGridView1.DataSource = bndSource;

            for (int q = 0; q <= dataGridView1.ColumnCount - 1; q++)
```

```
                 {
     this.comboBox1.Items.Add(this.dataGridView1.Columns[q].HeaderText.ToString());
                 }
             this.textBox3.DataBindings.Clear();
             this.textBox3.DataBindings.Add(new Binding("Text", bndSource,
                 this.dataGridView1.Columns[1].HeaderText.ToString(), true));
             this.label1.Text = this.dataGridView1.Columns[1].HeaderText.ToString();

         }

         private void button4_Click(object sender, EventArgs e)
         {
             bndSource.MoveNext();

         }


     }
 }
```

Now that you have tried to do everything with some existing code, next you will have the chance to build a simple data entry form with your own navigation buttons.

Simple Data Entry Form

To do this, save and close the project you were working on and create a new Windows Forms Application project. In this example, I've called it SimpleDataEntryForm. You will be using the Northwind database again, and this is just a simple form to navigate through Invoice and Invoice Details records. Since this is just an example, we are going to use the bare-minimum number of fields. So, create a text box, two DateTimePicker controls, and labels for each. These will be for Order ID, Order Date, and Ship Date. Then, add five more text boxes with labels. These will be for the Order Details fields for ID, Order ID, Quantity, Unit Price, and Discount. Then, add two more text boxes with a label in the middle that says "of." Then add four buttons that say Next Parent, Next Child, Add New Order Detail, and Save Changes. How your form looks isn't that important, but Figure 3-2 shows you what mine looks like.

You will be adding a bunch of additional objects when compared to the previous example, and you will also be adding event handlers to determine when the form has been updated. In addition, since I will be introducing the DataSet object here, you will see how updates are handled differently there. Please note that you could add Previous, Next, Move First, Move Last, and a host of other buttons if you wanted. Those button click events are handled just like Next buttons—you would just call the corresponding navigation method.

The only special things you need to take care of on the form design is setting the Enabled property of the "ID" TextBox (textBox2 on my form) to False. You also need

Figure 3-2. The Simple Data Entry Form

to make sure that you put the button click events onto the right buttons. So, let's dig into this.

As in the other code, you need to add the line of code to use `System.Data.OleDb`, and you will need to add the following variables at the class level:

```
public string connString;
public string query1;
public string query2;
public OleDbDataAdapter orders_dAdapter;
public OleDbDataAdapter order_details_dAdapter;
public DataSet NW_Orders;
public OleDbCommandBuilder cBuilder;
public OleDbCommandBuilder cBuilder1;
public BindingSource orders_bndSource;
public BindingSource order_details_bndSource;
public Boolean saveprompt;
```

The new items to discuss here are the two data adapters, two command builders, two binding sources, the lack of `DataTable` objects as variables, and the `DataSet` object. Because this form is using a parent table and the related records in a child table, you need to have different variables for all of those items. In addition, there is also a Boolean variable to track when you need to prompt the user to save changes. For the most part, the various data objects are going to be doing the exact same things that they were doing in the other examples; the new step in the code is going to be when you add the `DataTables` to the `DataSet` and then set the relation between the tables.

The `DataSet` object is very handy when compared to the ADO/DAO objects that you would have used in Access. Typically in VBA and Classic VB programming, you would get related records through a join query or a parameterized query. In C#, the `DataSet` object lets you add any of the tables that you want to the one object. You can then show

how the parent records relate to the child records. By doing this, you can simplify the process of adding and updating related records. You can also show parent and child records on the same form and handle the navigation without having to resort to separate forms. It does make sense in most cases to have your form laid out in a way to accomplish that. But there are times when you might be storing some related data in a separate table where it won't matter to the end user. As an example, you might store phone numbers in a separate table but only want to allow editing of the primary phone number in your form. In those cases, you can have one form that shows all your data, and you can have a very simple form that you couldn't achieve with VBA or Classic VB.

There is certainly some complexity in setting up this data structure, but I think once you break down the steps you will find that it isn't too complicated. When I was learning this, the biggest challenge that I had was finding complete examples showing what I was trying to do. When I was learning Classic VB and VBA, I could usually count on a good example with the particular function, method, or event being used in context in a complete example that I could run. Often, when you are searching for the same thing in C#, you see a partial example that you may or may not be able to use as-is in your code.

When I built my first form using a DataSet with multiple tables that were related, it took me some time to figure out how to use all of the objects in the right way to make updating the database work, etc. As it turns out, the methods are the same, but how you call them and which overloads you use to make them work are different.

The next snippet of code is what you need to set-up the DataSet:

```
InitializeComponent();
saveprompt = false;
connString = "Provider=Microsoft.ACE.OLEDB.12.0;Data Source=C:\\users\\michael\
\documents\\Northwind 2007.accdb";
NW_Orders = new DataSet();
query1 = "SELECT * FROM Orders";
query2 = "Select * from [Order Details]";
orders_dAdapter = new OleDbDataAdapter(query1, connString);
order_details_dAdapter = new OleDbDataAdapter(query2, connString);

cBuilder = new OleDbCommandBuilder(orders_dAdapter);
cBuilder.QuotePrefix = "[";
cBuilder.QuoteSuffix = "]";
cBuilder1 = new OleDbCommandBuilder(order_details_dAdapter);
cBuilder1.QuotePrefix = "[";
cBuilder1.QuoteSuffix = "]";

orders_dAdapter.Fill(NW_Orders, "Orders");
order_details_dAdapter.Fill(NW_Orders, "Order Details");

DataColumn parentcolumn = NW_Orders.Tables["Orders"].Columns["Order ID"];
DataColumn childcolumn = NW_Orders.Tables["Order Details"].Columns["Order ID"];
DataRelation relation = new System.Data.DataRelation("OrderstoDetails", parentcolumn,
childcolumn);
NW_Orders.Relations.Add(relation);
```

When you break this down, you are writing the queries, setting the command builders (this creates the functions to Add/Update/Delete), filling the data adapters in the Data Set (you could also create DataTable objects and add them, but this is easier and eliminates the need for more variables), and then setting up the relations. I'm going to focus on the DataSet differences here.

Once you have created the new DataSet called NW_Orders, you are going to fill your data adapters in the DataSet. You do this with the line of code that reads:

```
orders_dAdapter.Fill(NW_Orders, "Orders");
```

If you remember or page back to the example in Chapter 2, you filled the data adapter right into the Data Table. In this case, you are filling in the parameter for the DataSet object that you are using and you set the name that you want to give the DataTable that you are filling inside the DataSet. The DataSet differences were already covered; now let's see how you set up the relations between the DataTables. Take a look at the following lines:

```
DataColumn parentcolumn = NW_Orders.Tables["Orders"].Columns["Order ID"];
DataColumn childcolumn = NW_Orders.Tables["Order Details"].Columns["Order ID"];
DataRelation relation = new System.Data.DataRelation("OrderstoDetails", parentcolumn,
childcolumn);
NW_Orders.Relations.Add(relation);
```

First, you are defining DataColumn variables for the parent and child columns. I called them parentcolumn and childcolumn just to make it easier follow what is going on. The next line of code is where you are setting up the relation. The overload we are using here has three items. First, you have a string name that you are giving to the relation. This is important, and you need to remember it because you will need to refer to it when you create the binding source for the child records. An interesting thing happens when you set the DataSet up in this way. First, you will still have access to the entire table of child records that will not be related. This is tricky because if you refer to the child DataTable directly when you are trying to access the records related to the parent table, you won't get what you expect. This becomes visually clear in the next chapter when you access the DataSets with the GUI. In that example, you'll see each table individually, and then you'll also see the child DataTable again inside the parent table. When you are trying to access the child records related to the parent, this DataTable inside the parent table is what you need to access.

Doing that is fairly simple—you just won't see many examples that show you explicitly how to do that with code. There are plenty of examples with the data controls, but I do think it's helpful to learn it this way, and there are times when you will want to do this with code instead of doing it at design time. Take a look at the following lines:

```
orders_bndSource = new BindingSource();
orders_bndSource.DataSource = NW_Orders.Tables["Orders"];
order_details_bndSource = new BindingSource();
order_details_bndSource.DataSource = orders_bndSource;
order_details_bndSource.DataMember = "OrderstoDetails";
```

This is pretty straightforward once you see it. You create a `BindingSource` object and set it equal to the parent `DataTable` that you have in the `NW_Orders` (`DataSet`) object. Then, you create the `BindingSource` for the child records. However, the change is that the `DataSource` for the child data binding is the parent `DataSource`. Then, you set the `DataMember` equal to the name (string) that you gave the `DataRelation`. And that's it—now you have two binding sources that you can use. When you increment the parent record, the child binding source will update with the related child records.

Next, you'll set up event handlers to determine when the current item you're working with changes and when the list changes (meaning changes that aren't happening to the current item). We will also be putting in a more generic handler to catch these events in order to make sure we prompt the user to save the data, but I wanted to also show these events because you will often want to do something when one of them happens. The code snippet follows:

```
order_details_bndSource.CurrentItemChanged += new
EventHandler(order_details_bndSource_CurrentItemChanged);
        order_details_bndSource.ListChanged += new
ListChangedEventHandler(order_details_bndSource_ListChanged);
```

You can do this for any event, so if you haven't had a chance to use these in the past, this is a very powerful thing to be able to do. You can watch for mouse events, keyboard events, property changes, etc., and then run code to do specific things based on what happened. Keep in mind that these types of event handlers have to be done in code because these objects don't exist on the form for editing. You will also see that we can set the event handler for groups of objects on the form instead of editing every one. We are going to do that shortly.

While you have now written many lines of code, it wouldn't do anything yet if you executed the program now. While you have binding objects that are full of data, the code binding that data to the text boxes and date pickers hasn't been written yet. If you are writing this yourself instead of using the downloaded source code, make sure that you watch the text box names because if yours are named differently, you will need to edit which gets bound to what data. The code to bind is very simple and follows here:

```
this.textBox1.DataBindings.Add(new Binding("Text", orders_bndSource, "Order ID",
true));
        this.dateTimePicker1.DataBindings.Add(new Binding("Text", orders_bndSource,
"Order Date", true));
        this.dateTimePicker2.DataBindings.Add(new Binding("Text", orders_bndSource,
"Shipped Date", true));
        this.textBox2.DataBindings.Add(new Binding("Text", order_details_bndSource,
"ID"));
        this.textBox3.DataBindings.Add(new Binding("Text", order_details_bndSource,
"Order ID"));
        this.textBox4.DataBindings.Add(new Binding("Text", order_details_bndSource,
"Quantity"));
        this.textBox5.DataBindings.Add(new Binding("Text", order_details_bndSource,
"Unit Price"));
        this.textBox6.DataBindings.Add(new Binding("Text", order_details_bndSource,
```

```
"Discount"));
            this.textBox7.Text = "" + (order_details_bndSource.Position + 1);
            this.textBox8.Text = order_details_bndSource.Count.ToString();
```

This code snippet is binding the Text property of each control to a specific field in either the parent or child data source. The last two lines are adding a count of child records and writing the current position. (The current position will always start at zero because it is a zero-based collection, so we add one and it will always start at one.) Each time you move through the child records, you will need to increment that counter. And each time you move to a new parent record, you will need to update the count.

For the final lines of code in the opening procedure, I want to catch any instance of a user physically going into a field. If he does that, I want to prompt him to save any changes that may have been made. There are a lot of ways to accomplish this, and I wouldn't do it in this manner in a real-world application. But what I wanted to demonstrate here is a way for you to apply an event handler to a group of controls without having to manually do it. If you had a form with 100 controls and you wanted to run certain events on groups of them, you would save yourself a lot of time by using this next piece of code:

```
foreach (Control tx in this.Controls)
        {
            if (tx.DataBindings.Count > 0 && tx.Name != "textBox1"
                && tx.Name != "textBox3" )
            {
                tx.Enter += new EventHandler(tx_Enter);
            }
        }
```

The code snippet above is looping through every control. It is using the && operator to signify an AND condition. The operator != is the inequality operator. So, that line of code is saying if this control has bound data and it isn't one of the ID fields, then put an event handler on that field that will run when the user enters that control. I only needed to test for **textBox1** and **textBox3** because **textBox2** isn't enabled. In this example, the event handler calls the **tx_Enter** procedure. I hope you can see how using three lines of code to accomplish this could be useful on a form with a lot of controls. The next lines of code are the event handlers. You could write all of them in one event handler, but I did this with separate ones because you might want to apply different lines of code, depending on the event. So, I wanted you to see how to assign different procedures. If you replaced those other procedure names with **tx_Enter** in the code, you could eliminate those other procedures:

```
        void tx_Enter(object sender, EventArgs e)
        {
            saveprompt = true;
        }

        void order_details_bndSource_ListChanged(object sender, ListChangedEventArgs e)
        {
            saveprompt = true;
```

```
        }
        private void order_details_bndSource_CurrentItemChanged(object sender,
    EventArgs e)
        {
            saveprompt = true;
        }
```

In these cases, you are saying: if any of these events are triggered, set the `saveprompt` variable to `true`. Before I show you how we use that variable, I first want to cover how you pass the changes in the form's bound controls to the database. This is done slightly differently than we've seen earlier:

```
        private void SaveChanges_Click(object sender, EventArgs e)
        {
            try {

                orders_bndSource.EndEdit();
                order_details_bndSource.EndEdit();
                orders_dAdapter.Update(NW_Orders, "Orders");
                order_details_dAdapter.Update(NW_Orders,"Order Details");
                saveprompt = false;

                MessageBox.Show("Record Updated");
            }
            catch (OleDbException f)
            {
                MessageBox.Show("Record Update Failed - Error Code " +
    f.ErrorCode.ToString() );
            }

        }
```

First, you again will want to put this code in a `try` ... `catch` statement so that if there are any problems saving the data, you can pass that information to the user. It could fail for any number of reasons, including failing validation and invalid field names (if you didn't set the `QuotePrefix` and `QuoteSuffix`). You can also trap specific exceptions. In this case, you are trapping any `OleDbException`, but you can have specific text for every kind of exception. The first steps in the saving procedure are to end the edits on both data sources. Then there is a specific order that you need to call updates in a parent/child `DataSet`: Delete Child Records, Add/Update/Delete Parent Records, and finally Add/Update Child Records. Since the users don't have the ability to delete records in this sample application, you will skip that step here. If you think about how you called the update methods in the previous examples, this is similar. But remember that you don't have a `DataTable` object described here. So, you will use a different overload method, which takes the `DataSet` object and then the name of the `DataTable` as a string. The slightly confusing part is that for the child table, you pass the Data Table name and not the name that you gave the relation. Once this completes, you will show the message to the user, letting her know that it updated. You could also do this by updating a text box like we did in the example in Chapter 1. You set the save prompt to false after the user clicks save so that if she clicks save and then clicks a navigation button before any additional editing, you won't prompt her again.

The next two procedures are the navigation procedures; if someone clicks one of those buttons, you will prompt the user to see if she wants to save before moving off of the current record if the **saveprompt** is true. The code here is very similar to code that you would have in Classic VB or VBA:

```
private void NextChild_Click(object sender, EventArgs e)
{
    if (saveprompt)
    {
        DialogResult x = MessageBox.Show("Do you want to save the data first?",
"Important", MessageBoxButtons.YesNo);
        if (x == DialogResult.Yes)
        {
            try
            {

                orders_bndSource.EndEdit();
                order_details_bndSource.EndEdit();
                orders_dAdapter.Update(NW_Orders, "Orders");
                order_details_dAdapter.Update(NW_Orders, "Order Details");

                MessageBox.Show("Record Updated");
            }
            catch (OleDbException f)
            {
                MessageBox.Show("Record Update Failed - Error Code " +
f.ErrorCode.ToString());
            }
        }
    }
        order_details_bndSource.MoveNext();
        this.textBox7.Text = "" + (order_details_bndSource.Position + 1);
        saveprompt = false;

}
private void NextParent_Click(object sender, EventArgs e)
{
    if (saveprompt)
    {
        DialogResult x = MessageBox.Show("Do you want to save the data first?",
"Important", MessageBoxButtons.YesNo);
        if (x == DialogResult.Yes)
        {
            try
            {

                orders_bndSource.EndEdit();
                order_details_bndSource.EndEdit();
                orders_dAdapter.Update(NW_Orders, "Orders");
                order_details_dAdapter.Update(NW_Orders, "Order Details");

                MessageBox.Show("Record Updated");
```

```
                }
                catch (OleDbException f)
                {
                        MessageBox.Show("Record Update Failed - Error Code " +
        f.ErrorCode.ToString());
                }
            }
        }
        orders_bndSource.MoveNext();
        this.textBox7.Text = "" + (order_details_bndSource.Position + 1);
        this.textBox8.Text = order_details_bndSource.Count.ToString();
        saveprompt = false;
    }
```

Breaking down this code is pretty straightforward, and both pieces of code are similar. First, you are prompting to save, and that code is exactly the same as the save procedure (except that you didn't need to change the saveprompt to false). The first if statement is checking if you need to prompt the user, and since that variable is a Boolean, you just need the variable. The second if statement is checking the user input, and the code only runs the save routine if the user selects Yes. Then, regardless of what the save prompt was or how the user answered the Save question, the binding source (parent or child, depending) is going to be incremented. Then the text boxes that let you know how many child records there are and the current position are updated. The last step sets the saveprompt to false because we have already prompted the user to save, so now we are waiting for the next change. Note that you are doing the navigation methods on the binding source. But this shouldn't lead you to believe that the binding source is equivalent to the recordset object in ADO/DAO, because while there are some similarities, they are very different. The specific differences are that the recordset objects generally are connected. The ADO.NET objects that you have been using here are loaded and then disconnected, which is why you must call the updates to the database explicitly.

The only part of the code that hasn't been covered here is the AddNew method for adding child records:

```
    private void AddNew_Click(object sender, EventArgs e)
        {
            order_details_bndSource.AddNew();

        }
```

This code snippet simply adds a new data row to the child data table. When you do that, the binding source automatically moves to that new record. You should notice that the linked field—in this case, the Order ID—is automatically populated with the current parent record's Order ID. You don't need to do anything special with this; when you navigate away or click Save, those changes will be committed to the database.

While this chapter covered a lot of information, it is hopefully presented in easily digestible chunks. Once you go through the examples, things become very clear. The hardest part of this type of application programming is knowing when to use each option that you have. Typically, there are 5 to 10 different ways to accomplish any given task. I'm hoping to show a way that works here, however, you should keep your eye out for other ways of doing these things. I'm not suggesting that any of the methods here are the absolute right methods, but they have been tested and they work.

The full code listing for this example follows:

```csharp
using System;
using System.Collections.Generic;
using System.ComponentModel;
using System.Data;
using System.Data.OleDb;
using System.Drawing;
using System.Linq;
using System.Text;
using System.Windows.Forms;

namespace SimpleDataEntryForm
{
    public partial class Form1 : Form
    {
        public string connString;
        public string query1;
        public string query2;
        public OleDbDataAdapter orders_dAdapter;
        public OleDbDataAdapter order_details_dAdapter;
        public DataSet NW_Orders;
        public OleDbCommandBuilder cBuilder;
        public OleDbCommandBuilder cBuilder1;
        public BindingSource orders_bndSource;
        public BindingSource order_details_bndSource;
        public Boolean saveprompt;

        public Form1()
        {
            InitializeComponent();
            saveprompt = false;
            connString = "Provider=Microsoft.ACE.OLEDB.12.0;
Data Source=C:\\users\\michael\\documents\\Northwind 2007.accdb";
            NW_Orders = new DataSet();
            query1 = "SELECT * FROM Orders";
            query2 = "Select * from [Order Details]";
            orders_dAdapter = new OleDbDataAdapter(query1, connString);
            order_details_dAdapter = new OleDbDataAdapter(query2, connString);

            cBuilder = new OleDbCommandBuilder(orders_dAdapter);
            cBuilder.QuotePrefix = "[";
            cBuilder.QuoteSuffix = "]";
            cBuilder1 = new OleDbCommandBuilder(order_details_dAdapter);
            cBuilder1.QuotePrefix = "[";
            cBuilder1.QuoteSuffix = "]";

            orders_dAdapter.Fill(NW_Orders, "Orders");
            order_details_dAdapter.Fill(NW_Orders, "Order Details");
```

```
            DataColumn parentcolumn = NW_Orders.Tables["Orders"].Columns["Order ID"];
            DataColumn childcolumn = NW_Orders.Tables["Order Details"].Columns["Order
ID"];
            DataRelation relation = new System.Data.DataRelation("OrderstoDetails",
parentcolumn, childcolumn);
            NW_Orders.Relations.Add(relation);

            orders_bndSource = new BindingSource();
            orders_bndSource.DataSource = NW_Orders.Tables["Orders"];
            order_details_bndSource = new BindingSource();
            order_details_bndSource.DataSource = orders_bndSource;
            order_details_bndSource.DataMember = "OrderstoDetails";

            order_details_bndSource.CurrentItemChanged += new
EventHandler(order_details_bndSource_CurrentItemChanged);
            order_details_bndSource.ListChanged += new
ListChangedEventHandler(order_details_bndSource_ListChanged);

        this.textBox1.DataBindings.Add(new Binding("Text", orders_bndSource, "Order
ID", true));
            this.dateTimePicker1.DataBindings.Add(new Binding("Text", orders_bndSource,
"Order Date", true));
            this.dateTimePicker2.DataBindings.Add(new Binding("Text", orders_bndSource,
"Shipped Date", true));
            this.textBox2.DataBindings.Add(new Binding("Text", order_details_bndSource,
"ID"));
            this.textBox3.DataBindings.Add(new Binding("Text", order_details_bndSource,
"Order ID"));
            this.textBox4.DataBindings.Add(new Binding("Text", order_details_bndSource,
"Quantity"));
            this.textBox5.DataBindings.Add(new Binding("Text", order_details_bndSource,
"Unit Price"));
            this.textBox6.DataBindings.Add(new Binding("Text", order_details_bndSource,
"Discount"));
            this.textBox7.Text = "" + (order_details_bndSource.Position + 1);
            this.textBox8.Text = order_details_bndSource.Count.ToString();

            foreach (Control tx in this.Controls)
            {
                if (tx.DataBindings.Count > 0 && tx.Name != "textBox1" && tx.Name !=
"textBox3" )
                {
                    tx.Enter += new EventHandler(tx_Enter);
                }
            }


        }

        void tx_Enter(object sender, EventArgs e)
        {
            saveprompt = true;
        }
```

```csharp
        void order_details_bndSource_ListChanged(object sender, ListChangedEventArgs e)
        {
            saveprompt = true;
        }


        private void NextParent_Click(object sender, EventArgs e)
        {
            if (saveprompt)
            {
                DialogResult x = MessageBox.Show("Do you want to save the data first?",
"Important", MessageBoxButtons.YesNo);
                if (x == DialogResult.Yes)
                {
                    try
                    {

                        orders_bndSource.EndEdit();
                        order_details_bndSource.EndEdit();
                        orders_dAdapter.Update(NW_Orders, "Orders");
                        order_details_dAdapter.Update(NW_Orders, "Order Details");

                        MessageBox.Show("Record Updated");
                    }
                    catch (OleDbException f)
                    {
                        MessageBox.Show("Record Update Failed - Error Code " +
f.ErrorCode.ToString());
                    }
                }
            }
            orders_bndSource.MoveNext();
            this.textBox7.Text = "" + (order_details_bndSource.Position + 1);
            this.textBox8.Text = order_details_bndSource.Count.ToString();
            saveprompt = false;
        }

        private void order_details_bndSource_CurrentItemChanged(object sender,
EventArgs e)
        {
            saveprompt = true;
        }


        private void NextChild_Click(object sender, EventArgs e)
        {
            if (saveprompt)
            {
                DialogResult x = MessageBox.Show("Do you want to save the data first?",
"Important", MessageBoxButtons.YesNo);
                if (x == DialogResult.Yes)
                {
                    try
                    {
```

```
                        orders_bndSource.EndEdit();
                        order_details_bndSource.EndEdit();
                        orders_dAdapter.Update(NW_Orders, "Orders");
                        order_details_dAdapter.Update(NW_Orders, "Order Details");

                        MessageBox.Show("Record Updated");
                    }
                    catch (OleDbException f)
                    {
                        MessageBox.Show("Record Update Failed - Error Code " +
f.ErrorCode.ToString());
                    }
                }
            }
                order_details_bndSource.MoveNext();
                this.textBox7.Text = "" + (order_details_bndSource.Position + 1);
                saveprompt = false;

        }

        private void AddNew_Click(object sender, EventArgs e)
        {
            order_details_bndSource.AddNew();

        }

        private void SaveChanges_Click(object sender, EventArgs e)
        {
            try {

                orders_bndSource.EndEdit();
                order_details_bndSource.EndEdit();
                orders_dAdapter.Update(NW_Orders, "Orders");
                order_details_dAdapter.Update(NW_Orders,"Order Details");
                saveprompt = false;
                MessageBox.Show("Record Updated");
            }
            catch (OleDbException f)
            {
                MessageBox.Show("Record Update Failed - Error Code " +
f.ErrorCode.ToString() );
            }

        }


    }
}
```

The biggest takeaway from this chapter should be using related data tables within a DataSet. There are specific actions you take in navigating the data in these data sets and in passing changes to the database. While this process in C# is certainly more challenging from a programming standpoint, I do think that it opens up some options that you don't have with a form/sub-form solution in Access. Also, there is nothing stopping you from drawing the controls on the form with a border that makes it look like a sub-form if you think that is what your users are expecting.

The other thing that you may have not noticed is that you can bind to different types of controls. As an example, you bound the date fields to a date/time picker control. You can bind to a CheckBox, ProgressBar, ComboBox, etc. While that isn't new, it also isn't something that you are giving up when you use C#.

In the next chapter, you will have the chance to use the built-in controls for data access. You will build a similar parent/child form and when you are done, you'll have two different ways to accomplish these tasks.

Creating Data Entry Forms with Built-In Controls

If you have built Access applications in the past, you know that forms in Access have a nice record navigation box at the bottom (if you don't shut it off) and that navigation box holds controls that allow you to move between records, add records, delete records, etc. If you have been using this, the inconvenience of not having that built-in functionality in form design will definitely be felt when developing in .NET. But the good news is that using the built-in navigation controls in C# is much easier than what you built in Chapter 4. Also, you will have the same type of control over the data as you had in the last chapter.

To get started, go into Visual Studio and create a new Windows Forms Application. I called mine UsingDataControls. Given the data that you will be working with, stretch the form to be a little wider and taller. Next, go to the top menus and select Data→Show Data Sources (or press Shift+Alt+D). You will see the box shown in Figure 4-1.

Click on the hyperlink that reads Add New Data Source... and you will see the dialog shown in Figure 4-2. You will have several options depending on what you have available with your configuration of Visual Studio. In this case, the choices were Database, Service, Object, and SharePoint. You will be using a database here, so select Database and click Next.

The next screen, Figure 4-3, allows you to choose the database model that you want to use. Your choices are Dataset and Entity Data Model. There are a lot of nice things that you can do with the Entity Data Model, particularly on large projects where you have a set of developers writing application code and another set working on the database storage schema. With the Entity Data Model, you can write code to access data without having to worry about how it is stored. That said, this example is going to use the Dataset because the Entity Data Model is outside the scope of this introduction. So, select Dataset and click Next.

Figure 4-1. No data sources, yet

The next screen is going to ask you to select your data connection. Click on the drop-down box and if you don't see the file *Northwind 2007.accdb*, click on New Connection and browse to that file and select it. Then hit Next. On the next screen, make sure the box is checked to save the connection string and click Next again.

The next screen you see is shown in Figure 4-4. Click on the triangle to the left of Tables and then check the boxes for Orders and Order Details. Then click Finish.

Your Data Sources box will now show the table information. If you expand the Orders table, you will see what I described in Chapter 3 and what is shown in Figure 4-5—the Order Details table also shows up as part of Orders. This is because there is a relationship setup in the database already that links Order Details to the Orders table, and it has Order Details as a child table. Now, you will see how easy it is to build a form. Just drag the fields that you want onto the form. Just make sure when you drag the fields from Order Details that you drag them from the child table and not from the main Order Details table on that form.

For this example, you should show the following fields: Order ID, Order Date, and Ship Date from the Orders Table; and ID, Order ID, Quantity, Unit Price, and Discount. While I realize that you would never do this without all the data, we are just trying to build something conceptual. If you want to drag more fields on, everything will still work.

When you drag the first control on the form, you will see that Visual Studio automatically adds the data navigation control. You should also take note that there is a default control that Visual Studio uses based on the data. But you can click the drop-down box and choose a different control if you would like. Once you drag the controls on, you should see something like Figure 4-6 if you press F5 to launch the form.

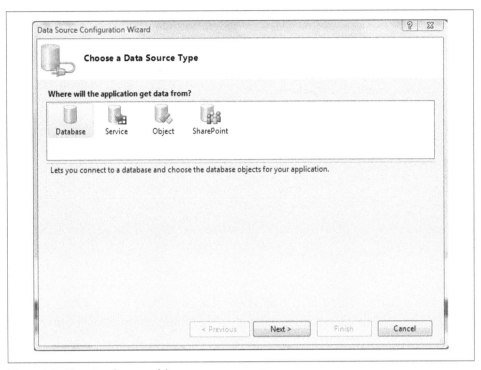

Figure 4-2. Choosing the type of data source you want

You will quickly notice that the navigation controls only control the parent data. If you go back into design view, you can add a second navigation control. Go to the Toolbox and scroll to the data section and select `BindingNavigator` and drag it onto your form. When you first drag it on, you will notice that you cannot move it. If you click on the triangle on the top right of the navigator, you will see the box shown in Figure 4-7. Check the Dock option to None. Then move the navigator above the Order Details controls. From there, right-click on the navigator and go to Properties. Find the `BindingSource` property and select `order_DetailsBindingSource`. If you press F5 and launch the form, you will notice that the data appears to work. If you were to go to the Order Details section and click Delete, the record appears to be deleted, but when you close and reopen, you will see that it didn't delete the data.

So, we are going to make some more changes. Some of the changes are for real functionality and some are just for show. Either way, they are all useful to learn. Click on the navigator on the top of the page and you will see a drop-down box appear. Click on that and select `ProgressBar`. Then right-click on the form and hit View Code, and from there you will write code to handle your updates, advance the progress bar, etc.

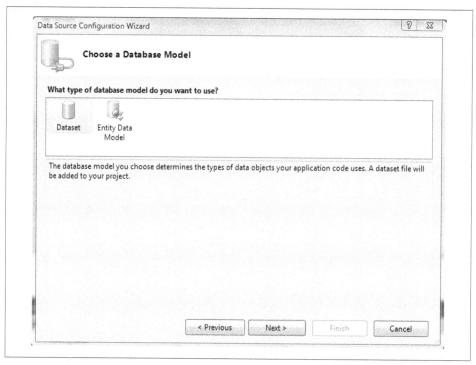

Figure 4-3. Choosing a model for your data source

There is already some code there for you, so you will just be adding some additional lines. In the `Form1_Load` procedure, you will add the two lines to set up the `Progress Bar`. See below:

```
private void Form1_Load(object sender, EventArgs e)
    {
        // TODO: This line of code loads data into the
'northwind_2007DataSet.Order_Details' table. You can move, or remove it, as needed.

this.order_DetailsTableAdapter.Fill(this.northwind_2007DataSet.Order_Details);
        // TODO: This line of code loads data into the 'northwind_2007DataSet.Orders'
table. You can move, or remove it, as needed.
        this.ordersTableAdapter.Fill(this.northwind_2007DataSet.Orders);
        this.toolStripProgressBar1.Value = this.ordersBindingSource.Position + 1;
        this.toolStripProgressBar1.Maximum = this.ordersBindingSource.Count;

    }
```

Note that the comments were added automatically by the controls. The last two lines in this are setting the position to the current position plus one. You need to add the plus one because position is zero-based. Then, you need to set the maximum value of the `ProgressBar` to the count of records in the DataSet (you are using a property of the binding source).

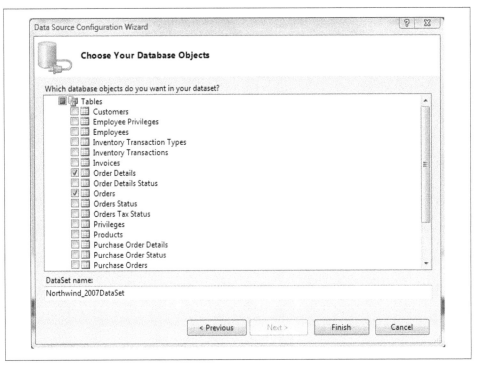

Figure 4-4. Choosing objects from the database

Next, go back to design view and double-click on the Save icon, which will bring you back to the code screen to write some code for save. You will see the following code already written there:

```
private void ordersBindingNavigatorSaveItem_Click(object sender, EventArgs e)
    {
        this.Validate();
        this.ordersBindingSource.EndEdit();
        this.tableAdapterManager.UpdateAll(this.northwind_2007DataSet);


    }
```

That code appears to work, and if you delete a record in the Order Details records and then click Save, it does indeed make that change in the database. However, if you edit a record in the details section and then click Save, it doesn't pass that along. This is because the EndEdit method is only being called for the parent. So, you just need to add the following line of code right before the UpdateAll method is called:

```
this.order_DetailsBindingSource.EndEdit();
```

While this works, you might decide to put a Save button on both navigators. That is entirely up to you. You might want to add code to check if data changed or add a

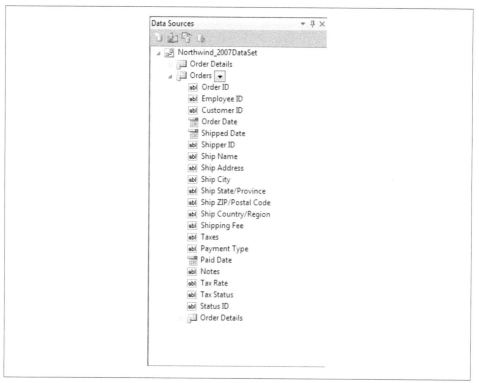

Figure 4-5. Data sources to choose from

confirming message when data is saved. We covered those items in the last chapter and the same concepts apply.

What isn't working right now is the progress bar. You could write code on every navigation button to add or subtract from the value to move the progress bar. But instead you can just apply something that you used in the last chapter. Add the following line as the last line in the Form1_Load procedure:

```
this.ordersBindingSource.PositionChanged += new
EventHandler(ordersBindingSource_PositionChanged);
```

This will add an event handler, and then you add one line of code into that, as shown below:

```
void ordersBindingSource_PositionChanged(object sender, EventArgs e)
    {
        this.toolStripProgressBar1.Value = this.ordersBindingSource.Position + 1;
    }
```

I hope you can see how using an event handler there is much better than trying to write code to catch actions by the users. Next, I want to draw your attention to the bottom of the form in design view.

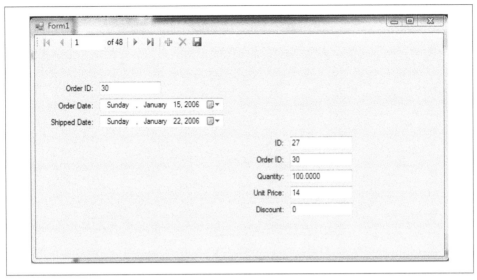

Figure 4-6. Form with controls added

BindingNavigator Tasks

Embed in ToolStripContainer

Insert Standard Items

RenderMode:	ManagerRenderMode ▼
Dock:	Top ▼
GripStyle:	Visible ▼

Edit Items...

Figure 4-7. Navigator details

In Figure 4-8, take a look at the objects below the form. You should notice that you have a DataSet, BindingSources, and TableAdapters. These are the same items you wrote with code in the previous chapter. The main difference is that you didn't need to write a ton of code to use these items. Visual Studio is handling all of that for you.

The next thing to try is editing the DataSet with Designer. On the Data Sources box at the very top, the second icon in looks like a triangle with two rectangles. If you hover over it, it should say "Edit DataSet with Designer." If you click on that, you will see a new tab open called *Northwind_2001DataSet.xsd*. See Figure 4-9.

If you right-click on the line between the two tables and click Edit Relation, the screen in Figure 4-10 will open up.

The Northwind Database already had relationships built. However, you can't always count on that happening with all databases. So, if you ever want to relate two tables

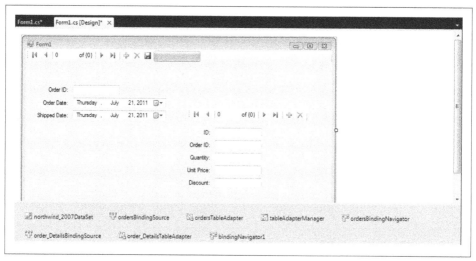

Figure 4-8. Objects lurking below the form

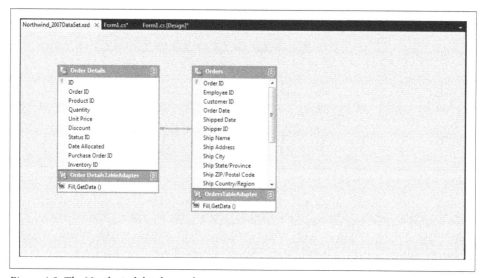

Figure 4-9. The Northwind database schema

that don't have a built-in relationship, you can do that here. You may also notice that at the bottom of the form, you can choose what to create. If you pick "Both Relation and Foreign Key Constraint," you have the ability to cascade updates and deletes to the child records. So, you could set it such that when you delete a parent row, it won't leave orphaned records in the child table. Whether you choose to do that is entirely up to you; I just wanted you to see where to do these things. Typically, you will be picking "Relation Only."

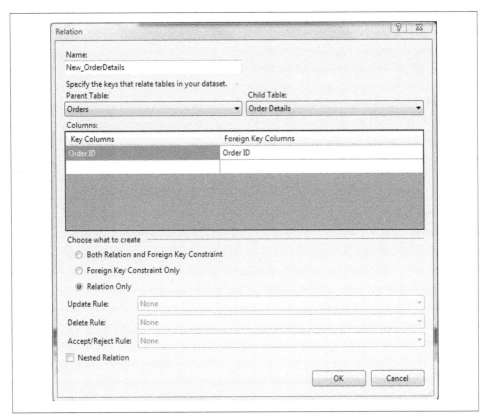

Figure 4-10. Editing the relationship between tables

In addition to this, if you right-click on a table, you can choose Configure. This brings up a screen where you can edit the query used to get the data. When you click Next, you can also choose what methods are built to deal with the data. If you take a look at the screen in Figure 4-11, you can see that you can uncheck the box to create the update methods. This can be useful if you want to create read-only access to the data. This way, you don't end up with a line of code that inadvertently updates or deletes data.

In Figure 4-12, you can see the completed form with the progress bar. I moved it partway through the data set so that you could see how the progress bar advanced. It is also worth noting that on the navigation bar, you can type in a record number that you want to go to, press Enter, and it will take you to that record.

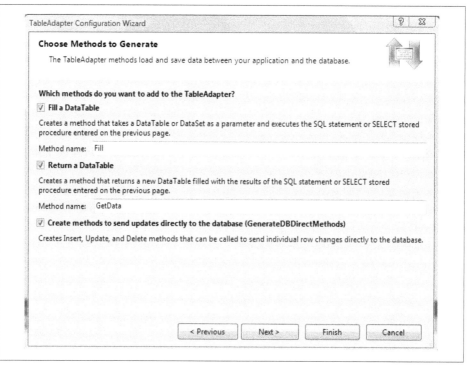

Figure 4-11. Boxes to control how much access is provided

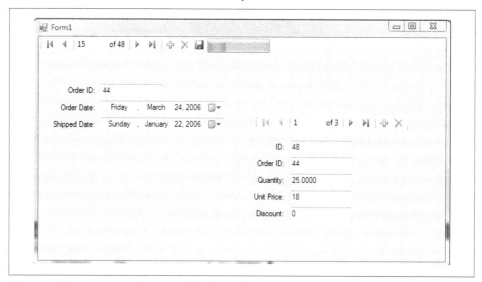

Figure 4-12. Jumping to a given record in the database

The full code listing follows here. Note that there is much less code in this one than in the previous samples. That is because most of the work is being done by the GUI, but you should have noticed that many more screen shots were used to demonstrate.

```
using System;
using System.Collections.Generic;
using System.ComponentModel;
using System.Data;
using System.Drawing;
using System.Linq;
using System.Text;
using System.Windows.Forms;

namespace UsingDataControls
{
    public partial class Form1 : Form
    {
        public Form1()
        {
            InitializeComponent();
        }

        private void ordersBindingNavigatorSaveItem_Click(object sender, EventArgs e)
        {
            this.Validate();
            this.ordersBindingSource.EndEdit();
            this.order_DetailsBindingSource.EndEdit();
            this.tableAdapterManager.UpdateAll(this.northwind_2007DataSet);

        }

        private void Form1_Load(object sender, EventArgs e)
        {
            // TODO: This line of code loads data into the
'northwind_2007DataSet.Order_Details' table. You can move, or remove it, as needed.

this.order_DetailsTableAdapter.Fill(this.northwind_2007DataSet.Order_Details);
            // TODO: This line of code loads data into the 'northwind_2007DataSet.Orders'
table. You can move, or remove it, as needed.
            this.ordersTableAdapter.Fill(this.northwind_2007DataSet.Orders);
            this.toolStripProgressBar1.Value = this.ordersBindingSource.Position + 1;
            this.toolStripProgressBar1.Maximum = this.ordersBindingSource.Count;
            this.ordersBindingSource.PositionChanged += new
EventHandler(ordersBindingSource_PositionChanged);
        }

        void ordersBindingSource_PositionChanged(object sender, EventArgs e)
        {
            this.toolStripProgressBar1.Value = this.ordersBindingSource.Position + 1;
        }
    }
}
```

The next chapter returns to SQL Server. There, you will be creating a web service and taking a parameter and returning a list. You don't need a hosting company to do the test, as an ASP.NET development server comes with Visual Studio. But if you wanted to, there are a couple of sites that will let you build a free test site with ASP.NET. You'll want to know the similarities and differences in data access between the desktop applications and web applications.

CHAPTER 5

Data in a Web Service

Writing a web service doesn't have to be a difficult or frustrating experience. I know many people, including myself, who struggled with writing one the first time. The challenge is more around understanding how different data types are returned and then taking care of the data access. I have written a simple example that will give you a great start toward writing one that will meet your needs.

The first thing that I want to cover is something called an SQL Injection Attack. When you are accepting input from users on the Web (really anywhere, but particularly on the Web), you need to be sure that you are taking precautions to avoid an SQL Injection Attack. In basic terms, if you are building an SQL Query String dynamically based on user input, a user can enter in text, end the first statement, then enter in malicious code (drop a table, overwrite data, etc.), and then put in a comment marker that would make SQL Server ignore the rest of the statement.

So, while you may be tempted to take user input in a variable—which for now we'll call x—and concatenate it within your string, you should avoid doing that at all times. Here's what it might look like in that example:

```
string x = (input from the user)
string sqlstr = "Select * from tbl_Test Where Product = '" + x + "'"
```

If you did that and someone targeted your site, all your data could be deleted. There are two steps that you can take to keep from being attacked in this manner. The first thing you can do is create a parameterized query. The second thing you need to do is validate the data in that parameter. Working with SQL Server parameters in C# is relatively straightforward. The part that you should keep your eye on is the data validation. Here's what the SQL string would look like if you changed it to take a parameter:

```
string sqlstr = "Select * from tbl_Test Where Product = @Product"
```

Now that we've covered that very briefly, I encourage you to read up on this type of attack before you take a site live, because these attacks impact websites all the time. Also, it should be noted that this logic applies to any website, not just a web service. You'll also see that a lot of people suggest using a stored procedure instead of a query

Figure 5-1. Setting up an empty web application

to access data. While I agree with that, it is difficult to write an application that isn't using some level of dynamic code for data access. Just keep a lookout for where you can use a stored procedure when you are building applications and when you can't make sure that you are using parameters. In addition, you should use strongly typed parameters so a malicious user or just a regular user in error can't put unexpected parameters into your query.

Writing a Web Service

Up through .NET Framework 3.5, a Web Service was a type of project that you could create. In .NET Framework 4.0, that option no longer exists. However, if you need to build one in .NET 4.0, you can simply create an Empty .NET Web Application and then add a Web Service as a Project Item.

Let's start by writing a simple web service, and then we can go through getting it data connected. To do this, open up Visual Studio (either the Full Version, or if you are using the Express editions, you would use Visual Web Developer) and go to File→New→Project, choose Web on the left, and then choose ASP.NET Empty Web Application. You will see a screen that looks similar to the one in Figure 5-1.

In this example, I called the project Chapter5_WebService. From here, go into Solution Explorer and you will see that there aren't many items in the lists. This is because we've started with an empty web application. To add in a web service, go to Project→Add

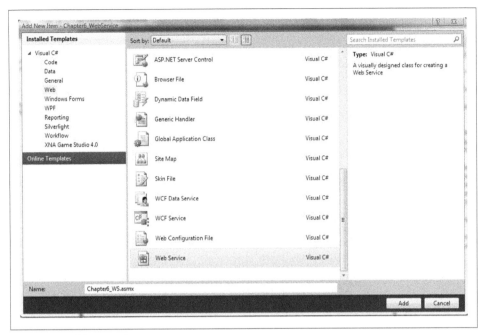

Figure 5-2. Adding a web service

New Item and you will get a screen like you see in Figure 5-2. Choose Web Service and give it a name. I've called mine Chapter5_WS.

In the top section of the code that opens, you will need to add references to be able to access data in SQL Server. In addition, you will be using a connection string set in the *Web.config* file, so you will need to add a reference to be able to access that. You should have the following lines of code at the top of your web service:

```
using System;
using System.Collections.Generic;
using System.Data;
using System.Data.SqlClient;
using System.Linq;
using System.Web;
using System.Web.Services;
using System.Configuration;
```

From here, you can change the namespace for your web service and add comments. For this example, the only change I made was to make the namespace chapter5_ws. The next piece of code can be added above the HelloWorld example supplied by Visual Studio, or you can replace that example with this code:

```
[WebMethod]
        public System.Collections.ObjectModel.Collection<string> listTest(string
thisList)
        {
            System.Collections.ObjectModel.Collection<string> holder = new
System.Collections.ObjectModel.Collection<string>();
            switch (thisList)
            {
                case "First":

                    holder.Add("one");
                    holder.Add("two");
                    holder.Add("three");
                    return holder;

                case "Second":
                    holder.Add("four");
                    holder.Add("five");
                    holder.Add("six");
                    holder.Add("seven");
                    return holder;
                default:
                    holder.Add("Invalid");
                    return holder;

            }
        }
```

Breaking down what this web service will do is pretty simple. You are writing a service that will take a string input and return a collection of strings. In this case, if the user passes First as the parameter, the service will return one, two, and three. If the user passes Second as the parameter, the service will return four, five, six, and seven. If the user passes any other parameter, the service will return invalid.

So, take that code and press F5 to launch the web service. The ASP.NET Development server will launch and show you a page with the services available listed as shown in Figure 5-3. Click on listTest and you will see a screen like the one shown in Figure 5-4. In the text box, enter Second and click the Invoke button.

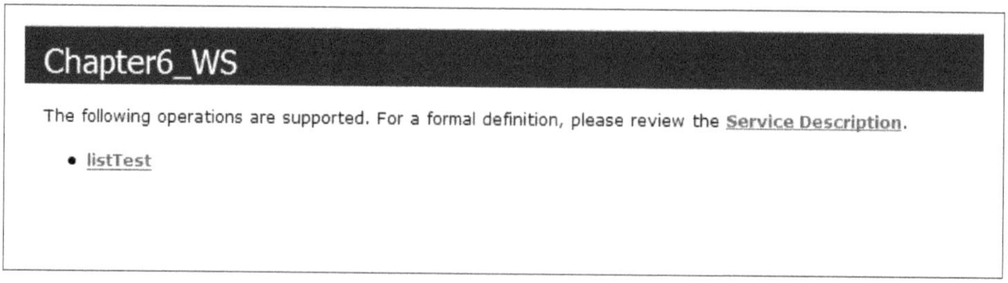

Chapter6_WS

The following operations are supported. For a formal definition, please review the **Service Description**.

- **listTest**

Figure 5-3. Launching a web service

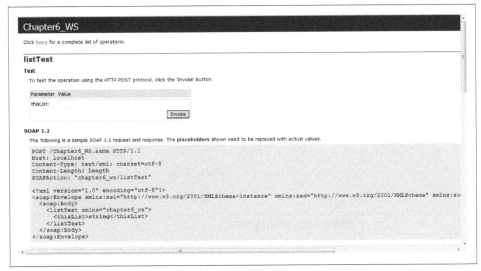

Figure 5-4. Entering parameters to test the service

Your browser will return the following XML:

```
<?xml version="1.0" encoding="UTF-8"?>
<ArrayOfString xmlns="chapter6_ws" xmlns:xsd="http://www.w3.org/2001/XMLSchema"
xmlns:xsi="http://www.w3.org/2001/XMLSchema-instance">
<string>four</string>
<string>five</string>
<string>six</string>
<string>seven</string>
</ArrayOfString>
```

This example isn't very useful on its own, but in a real-world application, you could pass a parameter to a web service and return a list to show on a drop-down list or something along those lines. Again, this one is static, but I'm showing it here so that you can see how a web service is written and called. Now, we need some data.

To accomplish this, go to Solution Explorer and right-click on the project name, then go to Add→Add ASP.NET Folder→App_Data. This will add the App_Data folder, which we will use to put in an SQL Server Database. See Figure 5-5 below.

Next, right-click on the App_Data folder and choose Add→New Item. This will bring up the screen shown in Figure 5-6. Choose SQL Server Database. In this case, I've named it WS_Database.

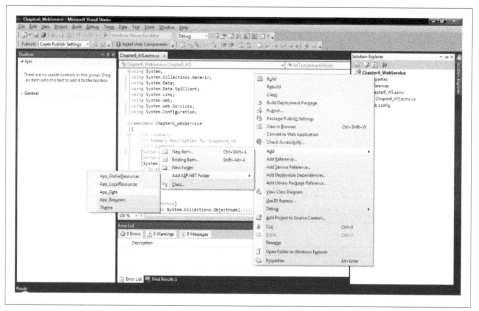

Figure 5-5. Navigating to App_Data

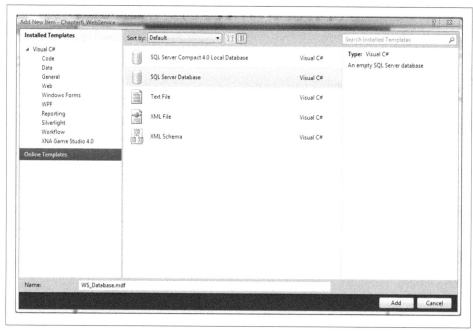

Figure 5-6. Choosing the kind of database

If you choose View→Server Explorer, you will see the SQL Server database that you created. This database's file will be in the App_Data folder of your application. If you click on the triangle to the left of the database, it will expand the database to show the objects. From there, right-click on Tables and choose Add New Table. You will see a screen like the one shown in Figure 5-7. Add the data fields shown there. Take note that the Product_ID is set to be the Identity Column.

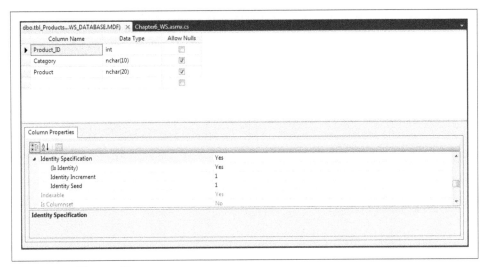

Figure 5-7. Adding a table

Once you have done this, click Save and save the table as **tbl_Products**. That is the only table that we are going to have in this database. In the example, I added several products, put Fruits or Vegetables as the categories, and put in the names of some fruits and vegetables as the product names. Now that it is saved, right-click on the table name and choose Show Table Data. Enter in a few rows of data. Figure 5-8 shows the rows that I added.

Product_ID	Category	Product
1	Fruits	Apples
2	Fruits	Bananas
3	Vegetables	Green Peppers
4	Vegetables	Celery
5	Vegetables	Carrots
6	Fruits	Melon
7	Vegetables	Beets
NULL	NULL	NULL

Figure 5-8. Adding some data

The next thing you need to do is add a few lines into your *Web.Config* file to store the database connection information. Your *Web.Config* file should look like the code below:

```
<?xml version="1.0"?>

<!--
  For more information on how to configure your ASP.NET application, please visit
  http://go.microsoft.com/fwlink/?LinkId=169433
  -->

<configuration>

    <system.web>
        <compilation debug="true" targetFramework="4.0" />
    </system.web>

    <connectionStrings>
        <add name="WS_Data"
        connectionString="data source=.\SQLEXPRESS;Integrated
Security=SSPI;AttachDBFilename=|DataDirectory|\WS_Database.mdf;User Instance=true"
        providerName="System.Data.SqlClient" />
    </connectionStrings>


</configuration>
```

The only part that you should have had to add is the part for connectionStrings. This line is saying to use your SQL Server Express database called *WS_Database.mdf* that is in the App_Data folder. (Using |DataDirectory| lets you reference that folder instead of having to use the physical path.) It is also using Integrated Security. You could also have a database that needs a username and password, but for this example, this will do just fine. Save the changes to the *Web.config* file and go back to the web service code.

You will be writing a procedure that will return a DataTable of products based on the Category name that a user passes to the procedure. The code will look like the listing below:

```
[WebMethod]
        public DataTable getProducts(string Category)
        {

            SqlConnection sqlcn = new
SqlConnection(ConfigurationManager.ConnectionStrings["WS_Data"].ConnectionString);

            DataSet ds = new DataSet();

            string sqlstr = "Select Product from tbl_Products where Category =
@Category";

            SqlDataAdapter ws_sql_adapter = new SqlDataAdapter(sqlstr, sqlcn);
            SqlParameter param =
ws_sql_adapter.SelectCommand.Parameters.Add("@Category", SqlDbType.Char, 10);
            param.Value = Category;
```

```
ws_sql_adapter.Fill(ds, "Products");
DataTable dt = ds.Tables["Products"];

return dt;
}
```

In this code, you are connecting to SQL Server, sending a parameterized select command, and returning records. It sounds easy enough, but it is helpful to break it all down. First, because you have already defined a connection string called WS_Data in the *Web.config* file and you have set a using reference to System.Configuration, you can reference that connection string in code through the ConfigurationManager object. You could certainly enter in a connection string there, but it is much easier as you add multiple pages in a web application to reference the connection string. Also, if you do it this way and your connection string changes, you can change it in one place and it will be used everywhere.

Next, you are adding a new DataSet object. This should already be familiar to you from the earlier chapters. The connection string that we are using here is selecting the column Product from your table, where Category equals the parameter that is being passed.

In order to create the select command, you need to add an SqlDataAdapter object using the query string that you created and the connection that you created. Once you have done that, you need to add an SqlParameter object to the SqlDataAdapter object. There are several overloads for this object, but we are using the one that passes the name, the data type, and the length. Remember, we are passing this as a strongly typed parameter to avoid getting passed malicious code in a parameter.

Now that you have a parameter object, you set the Value of the parameter equal to the Category variable, which is the parameter that is passed when the web service is called. The final steps are just to use the data adapter to fill the DataSet and then to create a DataTable object and reference it to the table that you just filled in the DataSet. Once this is done, your last line just returns the DataTable to the user. When I first tried to build a web service to return data, I spent a lot of time trying to change the DataTable into a collection, array, XML, etc—basically anything that I thought would get passed to the browser as XML. But the nice part about the web service is that it will do this for you for most objects without you having to do anything extra. All you need to do is return the object that you created and the web service will render it as XML. It is amazing how sometimes you can spend an hour on something and end up with only 12 lines of code that does what you need.

Save your progress so far and press F5 to launch the web service. Once it opens, click getProducts on the web page, enter Fruits in the text box, and click Invoke. You will get the following XML response:

```
<?xml version="1.0" encoding="UTF-8"?>
<DataTable xmlns="chapter6_ws"><xs:schema xmlns="" xmlns:msdata="urn:schemas-
microsoft-com:xml-msdata" xmlns:xs="http://www.w3.org/2001/XMLSchema"
id="NewDataSet">
<xs:element msdata:UseCurrentLocale="true" msdata:MainDataTable="Products"
```

```
msdata:IsDataSet="true" name="NewDataSet">
<xs:complexType>
<xs:choice maxOccurs="unbounded" minOccurs="0">
<xs:element name="Products">
<xs:complexType>
<xs:sequence>
<xs:element name="Product" minOccurs="0" type="xs:string"/>
</xs:sequence>
</xs:complexType>
</xs:element>
</xs:choice>
</xs:complexType>
</xs:element>
</xs:schema>
<diffgr:diffgram xmlns:msdata="urn:schemas-microsoft-com:xml-msdata"
xmlns:diffgr="urn:schemas-microsoft-com:xml-diffgram-v1">
<NewDataSet xmlns="">
<Products diffgr:id="Products1" msdata:rowOrder="0">
<Product>Apples </Product>
</Products>
<Products diffgr:id="Products2" msdata:rowOrder="1">
<Product>Bananas </Product>
</Products><Products diffgr:id="Products3" msdata:rowOrder="2">
<Product>Melon </Product>
</Products></NewDataSet>
</diffgr:diffgram>
</DataTable>
```

This returned the data of the products that we put under the category of Fruits. If you close that tab in your browser and try to call it with a category that you don't have defined, you will notice that it gives you a blank DataTable. This is important, as you will see when you try the next example.

Close out the browser and go back to the code. The next piece of code that you'll write is going to get an individual category for a product, meaning that if you enter Apples, the system should return the word Fruits. The code to do that follows:

```
[WebMethod]
public string getCategory(string Product)
{

        SqlConnection sqlcn = new
SqlConnection(ConfigurationManager.ConnectionStrings["WS_Data"].ConnectionString);
        DataSet ds = new DataSet();
       string sqlstr = "Select Category from tbl_Products where Product = @Product";

        SqlDataAdapter DataCommand = new SqlDataAdapter(sqlstr, sqlcn);
        DataCommand.SelectCommand.Parameters.Add("@Product", SqlDbType.Char, 20);
        DataCommand.SelectCommand.Parameters[0].Value = Product;
        DataCommand.Fill(ds, "Products");
        DataTable dt = ds.Tables["Products"];
        string category = "No Records";
        if (dt.Rows.Count > 0)
        {
            category = dt.Rows[0].Field<string>(0).ToString();
```

```
        }
        return category;
    }
```

I want to point out a few items for you to notice here. First, we are passing back a single string and not a `DataTable`. The second thing to notice is that because the product can have more characters in the table than the category (it was setup to have a maximum of 10 characters for the category and 20 characters for the product), you have to state that in the parameter object. The final thing to note is that we need to make sure that the query returns data. If you refer to `dt.Rows[0]` and there is no data, you will get an error. It is easy enough to check the count of the rows. So, rather than setting additional conditions, you can set the string that you are trying to return to "No Records." If a record is returned, you will overwrite that variable with the data in the first column of the first row that is returned. If you put a product in more than one category (in this example), this would only return the first record. You could make it return a `Data Table`, but I wanted to show an example where you would return an individual record. Start the web service and click on getCategory, enter in Apples as the product name, and click Invoke. You will get an XML response like you see below:

```
<?xml version="1.0" encoding="UTF-8"?>
<string xmlns="chapter6_ws">Fruits </string>
```

This web service would return "No Records" in place of "Fruits" if you entered a product name that wasn't in the database. Again, this is a relatively simple procedure, but I think it shows you some of the possibilities that you have and is a good example of how to work with an SQL Server database in a web environment. If you were to try this with your web-hosted site, you would need to make sure that ASP.NET 4.0 was enabled on the site, and you would need to change your connection string, as many web-hosting sites don't have the SQL Server in the same location. But, your web-hosting site will usually give you the connection string prebuilt, and you can just copy and paste.

There are a lot of APIs out there that you call as a web service. There are many different ways to call them in code. Typically, you would have an http post request and then you would look for the response, which is the XML that is returned. You can also use a SOAP request and response. When you run the web service in your ASP.NET development server and click on an operation, below the text box where you enter in your parameter(s), there are sample requests and responses for each type of request and response.

In a web application that you are building, you can easily call your web service by just creating a reference to it. To try this, go to Project →Add New Item and select Web Form, naming your web form **Default.aspx**. Enter the following code to make your web page, or you can go to the design view and drag the controls onto the page there:

```
<%@ Page Language="C#" AutoEventWireup="true" CodeBehind="Default.aspx.cs"
Inherits="Chapter6_WebService.Default" %>

<!DOCTYPE html PUBLIC "-//W3C//DTD XHTML 1.0 Transitional//EN" "http://www.w3.org/TR/
xhtml1/DTD/xhtml1-transitional.dtd">
```

```
<html xmlns="http://www.w3.org/1999/xhtml">
<head runat="server">
    <title></title>
</head>
<body>
    <form id="form1" runat="server">
    <div>

        Enter the category you would like to see:<br />
        <asp:TextBox ID="TextBox1" runat="server"></asp:TextBox>
       <asp:Button ID="Button1" runat="server" onclick="Button1_Click" Text="Button" />
        <br />
        <asp:GridView ID="GridView1" runat="server">
        </asp:GridView>
        <br />
        The count of the rows returned is:<br />
        <asp:TextBox ID="TextBox2" runat="server"></asp:TextBox>

    </div>
    </form>
</body>
</html>
```

Then, switch to code view and enter the following:

```
using System;
using System.Collections.Generic;
using System.Linq;
using System.Web;
using System.Web.UI;
using System.Web.UI.WebControls;
using System.Data;

namespace Chapter6_WebService
{
    public partial class Default : System.Web.UI.Page
    {
        protected void Page_Load(object sender, EventArgs e)
        {

        }

        protected void Button1_Click(object sender, EventArgs e)
        {
            Chapter6_WebService.Chapter6_WS wt = new Chapter6_WebService.Chapter6_WS();
            DataTable dt = wt.getProducts(this.TextBox1.Text);
            this.GridView1.DataSource = dt;
            this.GridView1.DataBind();
            this.TextBox2.Text = dt.Rows.Count.ToString();
        }
    }
}
```

This creates a simple web page that lets you enter in a Category, and when you click the button, it will populate a datagrid with the products. It will also populate a text

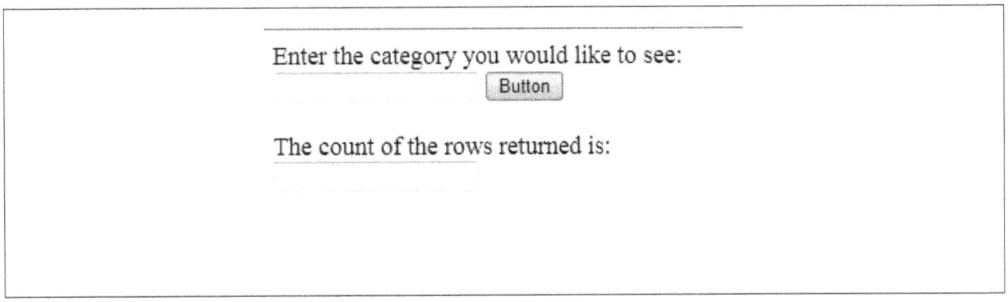

Figure 5-9. A simple web page for accessing the service

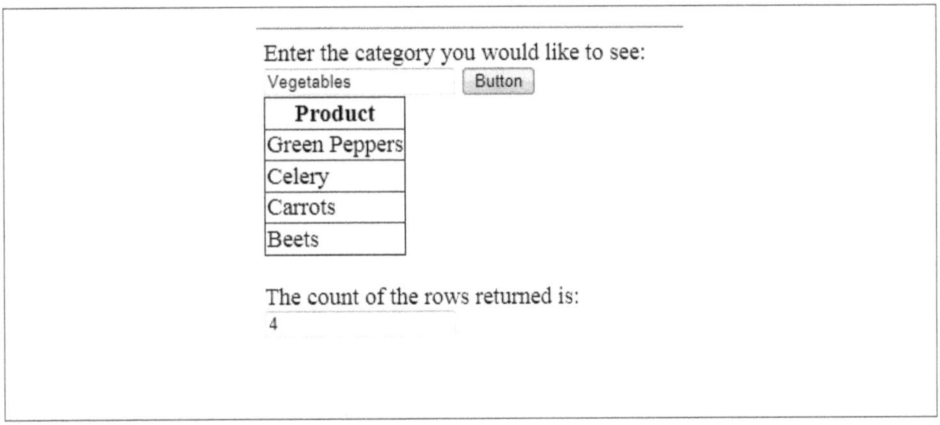

Figure 5-10. A response added to the web page

box with the number of rows returned. Figure 5-9 shows what the webpage looks like when opened.

Then enter in the word Vegetables in the top text box and click the button. Once you do that, you'll see the screen shown in Figure 5-10.

What is nice about doing this is you don't need to do anything special to take the response and put it in a DataTable. When the XML is returned, C# recognizes the type as a DataTable and you can bind it right to your datagrid. Also, note that the only addition to the "using" code is using System.Data;—everything else is already there by default.

You could also create a new website and, with your web service project running, go to Website→Add Service Reference, then enter in the address of your web service. In my case, the address bar shows: *http://localhost:63741/Chapter6_WS.asmx*. Once you enter that in, click Go. It will find that web service and you can expand it to see the operations in the web service. Before you click OK, rename the namespace for the reference to getData and then click OK. If you make the exact same web page as above, you just need to change the backend code to the code below:

```
using System;
using System.Collections.Generic;
using System.Linq;
using System.Web;
using System.Web.UI;
using System.Web.UI.WebControls;
using System.Data;
using getData;

public partial class _Default : System.Web.UI.Page
{
    protected void Page_Load(object sender, EventArgs e)
    {



    }
    protected void Button1_Click(object sender, EventArgs e)
    {
        getData.Chapter6_WSSoapClient wt = new getData.Chapter6_WSSoapClient();
        DataTable dt = wt.getProducts(this.TextBox1.Text);
        this.GridView1.DataSource = dt;
        this.GridView1.DataBind();
        this.TextBox2.Text = dt.Rows.Count.ToString();
    }
}
```

In this case, you are adding a line up top showing `using getData;`, which is setting a reference to the service that you added. You should notice that the way you create a reference to the service is slightly different in that you are referencing the `SoapClient`. But, other than those two changes, the rest of the code is identical. Also, please be aware that you have to have both projects running in order for this code to work. Typically, you won't be referencing your own web services in this manner. But, you will run into situations where you want to consume other web services, and I think it is much easier to add a service reference than it is to write your own SOAP or HTTP POST requests.

The code for the web service used was broken up into multiple pieces, so I'm showing the full code for the web service below. If you have a web service with multiple operations like this one, take notice of how the `[WebMethod]` line of code needs to appear above each. If you remove that line, there will be no errors in the code; it is just that an operation without `[WebMethod]` above it won't show up or be available on the web service.

```
using System;
using System.Collections.Generic;
using System.Data;
using System.Data.SqlClient;
using System.Linq;
using System.Web;
using System.Web.Services;
using System.Configuration;

namespace Chapter6_WebService
```

```
{
    /// <summary>
    /// Summary description for Chapter6_WS
    /// </summary>
    [WebService(Namespace = "chapter6_ws")]
    [WebServiceBinding(ConformsTo = WsiProfiles.BasicProfile1_1)]
    [System.ComponentModel.ToolboxItem(false)]
    // To allow this Web Service to be called from script, using ASP.NET AJAX, uncomment
the following line.
    // [System.Web.Script.Services.ScriptService]
    public class Chapter6_WS : System.Web.Services.WebService
    {

        [WebMethod]
        public DataTable getProducts(string Category)
        {

            SqlConnection sqlcn = new
SqlConnection(ConfigurationManager.ConnectionStrings["WS_Data"].ConnectionString);

            DataSet ds = new DataSet();

            string sqlstr = "Select Product from tbl_Products where Category =
@Category";

            SqlDataAdapter ws_sql_adapter = new SqlDataAdapter(sqlstr, sqlcn);
            SqlParameter param =
ws_sql_adapter.SelectCommand.Parameters.Add("@Category", SqlDbType.Char, 10);
            param.Value = Category;
            ws_sql_adapter.Fill(ds, "Products");
            DataTable dt = ds.Tables["Products"];

            return dt;
        }

        [WebMethod]
        public string getCategory(string Product)
        {

            SqlConnection sqlcn = new
SqlConnection(ConfigurationManager.ConnectionStrings["WS_Data"].ConnectionString);
            DataSet ds = new DataSet();
            string sqlstr = "Select Category from tbl_Products where Product = @Product";

            SqlDataAdapter DataCommand = new SqlDataAdapter(sqlstr, sqlcn);
            DataCommand.SelectCommand.Parameters.Add("@Product", SqlDbType.VarChar, 10);
            DataCommand.SelectCommand.Parameters[0].Value = Product;
            DataCommand.Fill(ds, "Products");
            DataTable dt = ds.Tables["Products"];
            string category = "No Records";
            if (dt.Rows.Count > 0)
            {
                category = dt.Rows[0].Field<string>(0).ToString();
            }
            return category;
```

```
        }

        [WebMethod]
        public System.Collections.ObjectModel.Collection<string> listTest(string
thisList)
        {
            System.Collections.ObjectModel.Collection<string> holder = new
System.Collections.ObjectModel.Collection<string>();
            switch (thisList)
            {
                case "First":

                    holder.Add("one");
                    holder.Add("two");
                    holder.Add("three");
                    return holder;

                case "Second":
                    holder.Add("four");
                    holder.Add("five");
                    holder.Add("six");
                    holder.Add("seven");
                    return holder;
                default:
                    holder.Add("Invalid");
                    return holder;

            }
        }
    }
}
```

What's Next

So far, you have had the chance to connect to Access and SQL Server in a desktop environment, and you've also connected to SQL Server in a web environment. In the next chapter, you'll build a simple web interface to edit records in an Access database. There are a lot of great web tutorials out there on using the MVC design pattern for websites, but getting into that depth is beyond the scope of this book. In this next example, we will be building a simple, one-page webforms site just to show how to access and edit data on a web page. We'll be using the Northwind database.

Editing Access Data on the Web

There are a lot of reasons why you might want to add or edit data on a web page. The example you'll go through in this chapter isn't really something that you would do in a real-world situation, but I want to introduce you to a couple of concepts that you'll find helpful if you need to interact with data through a web browser in the future.

It is worth noting that there are some great starter websites that you can build with Webmatrix. Currently, you can get Webmatrix on the Microsoft website (*http://www .microsoft.com/web/webmatrix/*), and from there you can install a prebuilt template to perform quick web development. Also, if you want to perform website functions like having a login, or if you want to use the MVC (model–view–controller) design pattern, you can use the preinstalled templates in Visual Studio. That said, it is still helpful for you to understand how to build a simple web page on your own.

In this example, you will begin with a blank ASP.NET website, as shown in Figure 6-1. I've called my website Chapter6. Note that you can do this from File→New→Web Site. If you want to build an MVC site, use File→New→Project and pick a Web project.

When you create this website, the only file in the website is *Web.config*. This means that you will need to add a Web Forms item to the website. To do this, go to Website→Add New Item and you will see a screen like the one shown in Figure 6-2. Call your web form **Default.aspx** and click Add.

Figure 6-1. Setting up an empty website

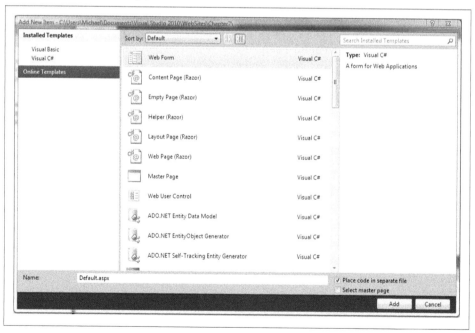

Figure 6-2. Creating a web form

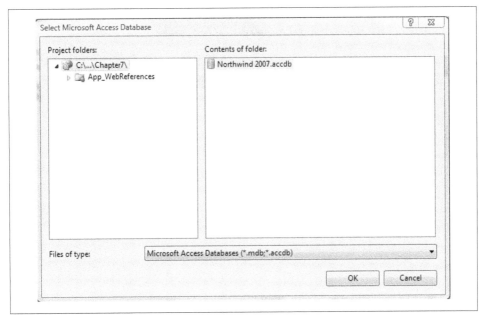

Figure 6-3. Choosing a specific database

We also want to create a reference to the Northwind database, and in this case, I want to put a copy of the Northwind database into the project. To do this, go to Website→Add Existing Item, select Data Files as the type, and navigate to where you have the Northwind database. Doing this will enable you to reference it at ~\Northwind 2007.accdb instead of having to add the entire physical path. Also, any changes that you make will happen in this copy and won't impact the normal database.

Now that you have added the database and the new web forms page, go edit the *Default.aspx* page in design view. At the top, type **Data from Customers table**. Then drag on a `GridView` control and an `AccessDataSource` control. Click on the `AccessData Source` object and go to Configure Data Source. When you hit browse, you will see a screen like the one shown in Figure 6-3. Click on the Northwind 2007 database and click OK. Notice how the file reference in Figure 6-3 shows the physical path. When you are working with files in C# in a web application, you can refer to the root directory with ~\, so I always recommend putting files into your project instead of trying to reference physical paths.

Once you click Next, you will get a screen like the one shown in Figure 6-4. On this screen, select the Customers table and leave the checkbox on the *. This will select all columns on the table. Then, click on Advanced and you will see the screen shown in Figure 6-5. Here, check the box to generate the Insert, Update, and Delete statements. Doing this will let you make changes to the table. Click Next and then click Finish. You can test the datasource on the last page if you wish, but generally you would only do that if you were writing a specific query, versus selecting an entire table. Also, please note that if you want the Insert, Update, and Delete statements, you must have the primary key field(s) selected in your query.

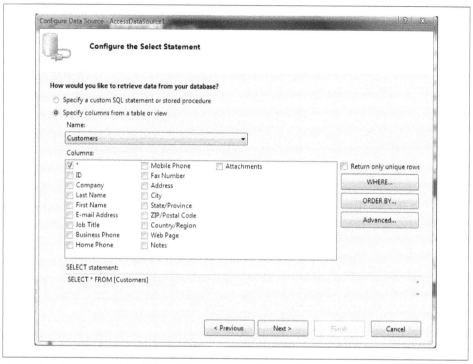

Figure 6-4. Choosing tables for the query

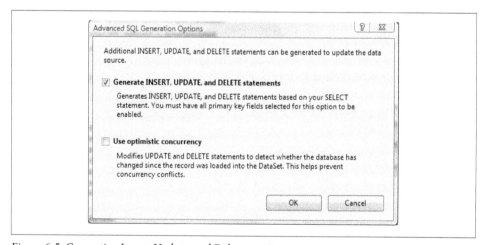

Figure 6-5. Generating Insert, Update, and Delete queries

Next, click on your datagrid and hit the > button on the top right of the grid. That will open up the GridView Tasks box, and you can set the options. For the datasource, select AccessDataSource1. Then check the boxes to enable Paging, Sorting, Editing, and Deleting. See Figure 6-6.

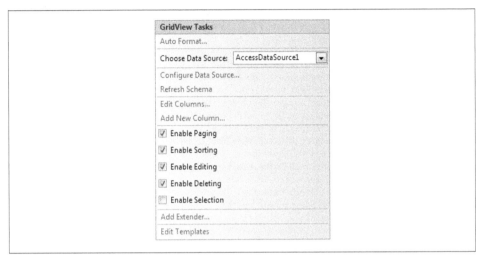

Figure 6-6. Choosing GridView configuration

Finally, click on Autoformat at the top of the GridView Tasks box. I selected Professional for mine, but you can pick whatever you'd like. At this point, it is ready to be opened. If you switch back to Source view on the web page, you will see the following:

```
<%@ Page Language="C#" AutoEventWireup="true" CodeFile="Default.aspx.cs"
Inherits="_Default" %>

<!DOCTYPE html PUBLIC "-//W3C//DTD XHTML 1.0 Transitional//EN" "http://www.w3.org/TR/
xhtml1/DTD/xhtml1-transitional.dtd">

<html xmlns="http://www.w3.org/1999/xhtml">
<head runat="server">
    <title></title>
</head>
<body>
    <form id="form1" runat="server">
    <div>

        Data from Customers table.<br />

        <asp:GridView ID="GridView1" runat="server" AllowPaging="True"
            AllowSorting="True" AutoGenerateColumns="False" CellPadding="4"
            DataKeyNames="ID" DataSourceID="AccessDataSource1" ForeColor="#333333"
            GridLines="None">
            <AlternatingRowStyle BackColor="White" ForeColor="#284775" />
            <Columns>
                <asp:CommandField ShowDeleteButton="True" ShowEditButton="True" />
```

```
<asp:BoundField DataField="ID" HeaderText="ID" InsertVisible="False"
    ReadOnly="True" SortExpression="ID" />
<asp:BoundField DataField="Company" HeaderText="Company"
    SortExpression="Company" />
<asp:BoundField DataField="Last Name" HeaderText="Last Name"
    SortExpression="Last Name" />
<asp:BoundField DataField="First Name" HeaderText="First Name"
    SortExpression="First Name" />
<asp:BoundField DataField="E-mail Address" HeaderText="E-mail Address"
    SortExpression="E-mail Address" />
<asp:BoundField DataField="Job Title" HeaderText="Job Title"
    SortExpression="Job Title" />
<asp:BoundField DataField="Business Phone" HeaderText="Business Phone"
    SortExpression="Business Phone" />
<asp:BoundField DataField="Home Phone" HeaderText="Home Phone"
    SortExpression="Home Phone" />
<asp:BoundField DataField="Mobile Phone" HeaderText="Mobile Phone"
    SortExpression="Mobile Phone" />
<asp:BoundField DataField="Fax Number" HeaderText="Fax Number"
    SortExpression="Fax Number" />
<asp:BoundField DataField="Address" HeaderText="Address"
    SortExpression="Address" />
<asp:BoundField DataField="City" HeaderText="City"
SortExpression="City" />
<asp:BoundField DataField="State/Province" HeaderText="State/Province"
    SortExpression="State/Province" />
<asp:BoundField DataField="ZIP/Postal Code" HeaderText="ZIP/Postal Code"
    SortExpression="ZIP/Postal Code" />
<asp:BoundField DataField="Country/Region" HeaderText="Country/Region"
    SortExpression="Country/Region" />
<asp:BoundField DataField="Web Page" HeaderText="Web Page"
    SortExpression="Web Page" />
<asp:BoundField DataField="Notes" HeaderText="Notes"
SortExpression="Notes" />
<asp:BoundField DataField="Attachments" HeaderText="Attachments"
    SortExpression="Attachments" />
</Columns>
<EditRowStyle BackColor="#999999" />
<FooterStyle BackColor="#5D7B9D" Font-Bold="True" ForeColor="White" />
<HeaderStyle BackColor="#5D7B9D" Font-Bold="True" ForeColor="White" />
<PagerStyle BackColor="#284775" ForeColor="White"
    HorizontalAlign="Center" />
<RowStyle BackColor="#F7F6F3" ForeColor="#333333" />
<SelectedRowStyle BackColor="#E2DED6" Font-Bold="True"
    ForeColor="#333333" />
<SortedAscendingCellStyle BackColor="#E9E7E2" />
<SortedAscendingHeaderStyle BackColor="#506C8C" />
<SortedDescendingCellStyle BackColor="#FFFDF8" />
<SortedDescendingHeaderStyle BackColor="#6F8DAE" />
</asp:GridView>

<asp:AccessDataSource ID="AccessDataSource1" runat="server"
    DataFile="~/Northwind 2007.accdb"
    DeleteCommand="DELETE FROM [Customers] WHERE [ID] = ?"
    InsertCommand="INSERT INTO [Customers] ([ID], [Company], [Last Name], [First
```

```
Name], [E-mail Address], [Job Title], [Business Phone], [Home Phone], [Mobile Phone],
[Fax Number], [Address], [City], [State/Province], [ZIP/Postal Code], [Country/
Region], [Web Page], [Notes], [Attachments]) VALUES
(?, ?, ?, ?, ?, ?, ?, ?, ?, ?, ?, ?, ?, ?, ?, ?, ?, ?)"
            SelectCommand="SELECT * FROM [Customers]"
          UpdateCommand="UPDATE [Customers] SET [Company] = ?, [Last Name] = ?, [First
Name] = ?, [E-mail Address] = ?, [Job Title] = ?, [Business Phone] = ?, [Home Phone]
= ?, [Mobile Phone] = ?, [Fax Number] = ?, [Address] = ?, [City] = ?, [State/Province]
= ?, [ZIP/Postal Code] = ?, [Country/Region] = ?, [Web Page] = ?, [Notes] = ?,
[Attachments] = ? WHERE [ID] = ?">
                <DeleteParameters>
                    <asp:Parameter Name="ID" Type="Int32" />
                </DeleteParameters>
                <InsertParameters>
                    <asp:Parameter Name="ID" Type="Int32" />
                    <asp:Parameter Name="Company" Type="String" />
                    <asp:Parameter Name="Last_Name" Type="String" />
                    <asp:Parameter Name="First_Name" Type="String" />
                    <asp:Parameter Name="column1" Type="String" />
                    <asp:Parameter Name="Job_Title" Type="String" />
                    <asp:Parameter Name="Business_Phone" Type="String" />
                    <asp:Parameter Name="Home_Phone" Type="String" />
                    <asp:Parameter Name="Mobile_Phone" Type="String" />
                    <asp:Parameter Name="Fax_Number" Type="String" />
                    <asp:Parameter Name="Address" Type="String" />
                    <asp:Parameter Name="City" Type="String" />
                    <asp:Parameter Name="column2" Type="String" />
                    <asp:Parameter Name="column3" Type="String" />
                    <asp:Parameter Name="column4" Type="String" />
                    <asp:Parameter Name="Web_Page" Type="String" />
                    <asp:Parameter Name="Notes" Type="String" />
                    <asp:Parameter Name="Attachments" Type="String" />
                </InsertParameters>
                <UpdateParameters>
                    <asp:Parameter Name="Company" Type="String" />
                    <asp:Parameter Name="Last_Name" Type="String" />
                    <asp:Parameter Name="First_Name" Type="String" />
                    <asp:Parameter Name="column1" Type="String" />
                    <asp:Parameter Name="Job_Title" Type="String" />
                    <asp:Parameter Name="Business_Phone" Type="String" />
                    <asp:Parameter Name="Home_Phone" Type="String" />
                    <asp:Parameter Name="Mobile_Phone" Type="String" />
                    <asp:Parameter Name="Fax_Number" Type="String" />
                    <asp:Parameter Name="Address" Type="String" />
                    <asp:Parameter Name="City" Type="String" />
                    <asp:Parameter Name="column2" Type="String" />
                    <asp:Parameter Name="column3" Type="String" />
                    <asp:Parameter Name="column4" Type="String" />
                    <asp:Parameter Name="Web_Page" Type="String" />
                    <asp:Parameter Name="Notes" Type="String" />
                    <asp:Parameter Name="Attachments" Type="String" />
                    <asp:Parameter Name="ID" Type="Int32" />
                </UpdateParameters>
            </asp:AccessDataSource>
            <br />
```

```
        </div>
      </form>
  </body>
  </html>
```

This is really handy if you are trying to make a web page that is identical to another web page. You can just copy the code and it will create the page. This isn't as easy to do in Microsoft Access or even in Classic VB. If you read through this, you will see that every option that you selected on your objects are shown here in the markup.

Before you add any code, open up this page and see what it looks like. Then click on the Edit link on the first row and you will see a page like the one shown in Figure 6-7. You can make a change to that row and then click Update to accept your changes, or click Cancel to discard your changes. Because you have enabled sorting, you can click on any of the column headings to sort the data on that column. Also, because paging is enabled, you can click on the numbers at the bottom of the page to page through the records.

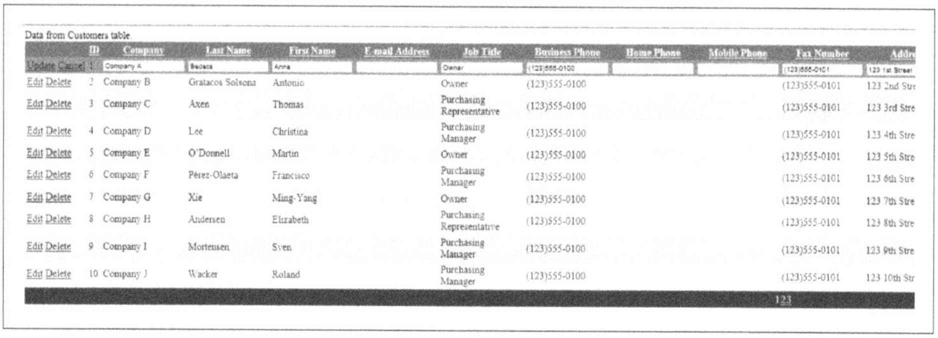

Figure 6-7. Web page in action, even without any code

Now that you have seen what happens with no code, close out the browser and go to the page again. On your datagrid, go to the GridView Tasks box and check the box to enable selection. Then, add a button and a text box at the bottom of the page in design view and then go to the code behind the web page. What you'll be doing here is customizing the look of the page somewhat. The first thing that you'll change is the page size. This sets how many records show on each page. Next, you will put code behind the button. It is easier if you go back to the design view and double-click on the button, as it will add the procedure, so you'll just need to edit it. For that button, you will be adding code to put some data from the selected record in the text box. That code will look like this:

```
using System;
using System.Collections.Generic;
using System.Linq;
using System.Web;
using System.Web.UI;
```

```
using System.Web.UI.WebControls;
using System.Data;


public partial class _Default : System.Web.UI.Page
{
    protected void Page_Load(object sender, EventArgs e)
    {
        this.GridView1.PageSize = 5;

    }

    protected void Button1_Click1(object sender, EventArgs e)
    {
        this.TextBox1.Text = "No Record Selected";
        if (this.GridView1.SelectedRow != null)
        {
            this.TextBox1.Text = this.GridView1.SelectedRow.Cells[3].Text.ToString();
        }

    }
}
```

When the page loads, the grid will be updated to only show five records at a time. If you click on the button and haven't selected a record, it will put "No Record Selected" in the text box. If a record is selected, it will put the third column (last name) in the text box. See Figure 6-8.

Data from Customers table.

		ID	Company	Last Name	First Name	E-mail Address	Job Title	Business Phone	Home Phone	Mobile Phone	Fax Number	Address	City	State/Province	ZIP/Postal Code
Edit	Delete	Select	21	Company U	Tham	Bernard		Accounting Manager	(123)555 -0100			(123) 555- 0101	789 21th Street	Minneapolis	MN	99999
Edit	Delete	Select	22	Company V	Ramos	Luciana		Purchasing Assistant	(123)555 -0100			(123) 555- 0101	789 22th Street	Milwaukee	WI	99999
Edit	Delete	Select	23	Company W	Entin	Michael		Purchasing Manager	(123)555 -0100			(123) 555- 0101	789 23th Street	Portland	OR	99999
Edit	Delete	Select	24	Company X	Hasselberg	Jonas		Owner	(123)555 -0100			(123) 555- 0101	789 24th Street	Salt Lake City	UT	99999
Edit	Delete	Select	25	Company Y	Rodman	John		Purchasing Manager	(123)555 -0100			(123) 555- 0101	789 25th Street	Chicago	IL	99999

123456

Button Tham

Figure 6-8. The updated web table

To show you how you can catch an event, add the following code into the page open procedure and then add the event code shown below:

```
protected void Page_Load(object sender, EventArgs e)
    {
        this.GridView1.PageSize = 5;
        GridView1.SelectedIndexChanged += new
EventHandler(GridView1_SelectedIndexChanged);
    }

    void GridView1_SelectedIndexChanged(object sender, EventArgs e)
    {
        this.TextBox1.Text = this.GridView1.SelectedRow.Cells[2].Text.ToString();
    }
```

This code will put the Company name (column 2) in the text box when you select a record, and if you press the button, it will put the last name (column 3) into the text box. I'm showing you this because you could use code like this to show details for an item. As an example, you might have a query showing customer invoices. Then you might want to add code to populate a datagrid with invoice details when you click Select. That would be a better user experience than having to select a record and then also click a button. But, there are other times where you might want to do something only when a button is clicked—maybe something like calling a web service to check on the shipping status of an order.

In any case, you can see with this example that it is possible to create a usable form with out-of-the-box controls and very little code. While you probably won't do anything exactly like this example, hopefully this demonstrates how to accomplish these tasks. As an additional note, you could easily substitute the AccessDataSource control for an SQLDataSource, XmlDataSource, EntityDataSource, etc., and use those for the datagrid.

What's Next?

If you look back at the goals in Chapter 1, all those topics and a few others have been covered. In the next chapter, I will review the key concepts and discuss some other possibilities. In addition, you will see some additional resources that will help you. Most programmers I speak with just need a working example of something that is close to what they want to do—they can run with it from there.

CHAPTER 7

Additional C# and Database Topics

There are a few other items in C# that you will find useful as you start to build applications—whether online or on the desktop. In this chapter, you can add some additional code to the projects that you've already built (or downloaded), or you can just put the extra code into a new project.

Referring to Connection Strings

If you think back to the Windows Forms applications that you worked on earlier, you would often have a line that looked like:

```
connString = "Provider=Microsoft.ACE.OLEDB.12.0;Data
    Source=C:\\users\\michael\\documents\\Northwind 2007.accdb";
```

While this is fine to do, if you had database connections on multiple forms and then you wanted to point to a different database, you would have a lot of changes to make. You may have noticed in the ASP.NET application that there was always a *Web.config* file that could hold the connection strings, among other settings. Well, you have the ability to create a similar file in your Windows Forms applications to do the same thing.

To do this, go to Project→Add New Item and select Application Configuration File, then leave the file name as *App.Config* and press Add. Then edit the *App.Config* file and enter the lines that you see below:

```
<?xml version="1.0" encoding="utf-8" ?>
<configuration>
    <connectionStrings>
        <add name="NW_Data" connectionString="Provider=Microsoft.ACE.OLEDB.12.0;Data
Source=C:\users\michael\documents\Northwind 2007.accdb"/>
    </connectionStrings>
</configuration>
```

Then, either add a new Windows Form or edit a form you already have. Put on a button and add the following code in the button_click event:

```
MessageBox.Show(ConfigurationManager.ConnectionStrings["NW_Data"].ConnectionString,
"Connection String", MessageBoxButtons.OK);
        OleDbDataAdapter dadapter = new OleDbDataAdapter("Select * from Customers",
ConfigurationManager.ConnectionStrings["NW_Data"].ConnectionString);
        DataTable dt = new DataTable();
        dadapter.Fill(dt);
        MessageBox.Show(dt.Rows.Count.ToString(), "Row Count",
MessageBoxButtons.OK);
```

This code will show you a message box with the connection string that you put in your
App.Config file, then it will open the Customers table and show you a message box with
the row count. If you see errors when you enter the code above, you will need to make
sure the following lines are in the top section of the code:

```
using System.Data;
using System.Data.OleDb;
using System.Configuration;
If you enter these lines and still see an error (particularly on the
ConfigurationManager line), make sure that you have a reference to
System.Configuration in your project. You do this by going to Project > Add Reference
and then click on the .Net tab as seen in Figure 7-1. Then, find System.Configuration
and click on it and then press OK. You code will run properly then.
```

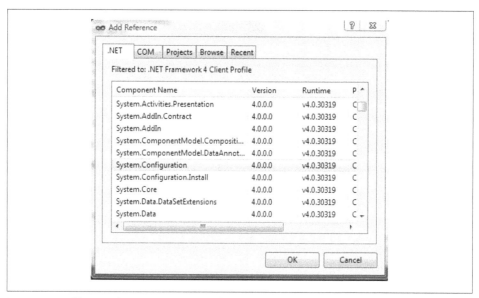

Figure 7-1. Adding a reference to System.Configuration

It is also possible to have multiple connection strings in the *App.Config* file, and you
can loop through the connection strings. There are a couple of objects you need to use.
Take a look at the code below:

```
        private void button1_Click(object sender, EventArgs e)
        {
            ConnectionStringSettingsCollection csc =
ConfigurationManager.ConnectionStrings;
            if (csc != null)
            {
                foreach (ConnectionStringSettings connstr in csc)
                {
                    MessageBox.Show(connstr.ConnectionString, connstr.Name,
MessageBoxButtons.OK);
                    var result = MessageBox.Show("Do you want to open?", "Question",
MessageBoxButtons.YesNo);
                    if (result == DialogResult.Yes)
                    {
                        OleDbDataAdapter dadapter = new OleDbDataAdapter("Select * from
Customers", connstr.ConnectionString);
                        DataTable dt = new DataTable();
                        dadapter.Fill(dt);
                        MessageBox.Show(dt.Rows.Count.ToString(), "Row Count",
MessageBoxButtons.OK);
                    }
                }
            }


        }
```

It isn't likely that you will have a Customer table in each database, but this is just for demonstration. Also, you will see that I have included a MessageBox to ask if you want to open the connection. I did that because there is a default LocalSqlServer connection that may show up for you that isn't going to be in your *App.Config* file. I say that it may show up for you because that connection is defined in the *machine.config* file when you install .NET Framework 4. You can also add other connections to that file if you want. In any event, I wrote this code in a way that lets you skip any connection that you don't want to open.

Also, it is worth noting that you should really only do your database connections in the *App.Config* file when you aren't using passwords (many Access databases), or when you are using integrated security. Any username or password that you show in that file will be viewable by the user if they know where to look. There are some good references online about encrypting data like this; however, that is outside the scope of this book.

Building Strings with Database Data

One of the items that I find myself doing quite often is passing data to the user in a string. For example, let's say that you have a table with customer data and you want to show the user data with the customer's name and phone number. Assume it should read: This customer's last name is Smith and the phone number is 800-555-1212.

You could build that with something like:

```
private void button1_Click(object sender, EventArgs e)
{
    ConnectionStringSettingsCollection csc =
ConfigurationManager.ConnectionStrings;
    if (csc != null)
    {
        foreach (ConnectionStringSettings connstr in csc)
        {
            MessageBox.Show(connstr.ConnectionString, connstr.Name,
MessageBoxButtons.OK);
            var result = MessageBox.Show("Do you want to open?", "Question",
MessageBoxButtons.YesNo);
            if (result == DialogResult.Yes)
            {
                OleDbDataAdapter dadapter = new OleDbDataAdapter("Select * from
Customers", connstr.ConnectionString);
                DataTable dt = new DataTable();
                dadapter.Fill(dt);
                DataRow dr = dt.Rows[2];
                string str = "This customer's last name is " + dr[2].ToString()
+ " and the phone number is " + dr[6].ToString();
                MessageBox.Show(str, "Info", MessageBoxButtons.OK);
            }
        }
    }
}
```

This will do the same loop as earlier, and you can see how the string is being built with the + operator. I have it looking at the third row (row 2 is the third row because the rows collection is zero-based). While that works, it can get difficult to work within a large string. You can change the second-to-last line to:

```
string str = string.Format("This customer's last name is {0} and the phone number is
{1}",dr[2].ToString(),dr[6].ToString());
```

This is taking advantage of the **string.Format** method. You refer to the data you want to reference with a zero-based index in curly braces right inside the string. That method will replace those references with the data you place after the string set off by commas. You can also reuse the same date field more than once and also use some built-in formatting. As an example, let's say that you want to reference the current time and you want to look at the hours and minutes independently. You could have a few lines of code like the following:

```
string clientName = "Michael";
string teststr = string.Format("The client's name is {0} and the current
hour is {1:hh} and the current minute is {1:mm}", clientName, DateTime.Now);
MessageBox.Show(teststr, "test", MessageBoxButtons.OK);
```

You can see that you reference the hours by hh and the minutes by mm, and you refer to the current date and time by using {1} for both spots. There are several ways that you can format your data, and you can also set an alignment setting that is optional. The layout of the reference is {index,alignment:format}. If you are skipping alignment, you eliminate the comma, and if you are skipping the format, you eliminate the colon. You can see all of the built-in formats by searching "Standard Numeric Format Strings" and "Standard Date and Time Format Strings" on MSDN.

Reporting

You may find it useful to perform reporting in an application. There is a report wizard in Visual Studio (not in Express), and you can show those reports in a ReportViewer Control. To use the report viewer, take a Windows Forms form and get to the design view. Then, open up the Toolbox and scroll down to the Reporting section. Drag the ReportViewer onto the form. You will get a menu that will ask you which report you want to show, or it will let you build a new report. There is a Report Definition Language (RDL) you can use to generate a report on the fly. This is very similar to the SQL Server Reporting Services. The difference is that the Visual Studio reports are RDLC files and saved and run locally, while the SQL Server reports are RDL files and they are saved and run remotely.

An entire book could be written on reporting, so I'm not going to go into great detail here. There is a fantastic walk-through on building a report on MSDN that I highly encourage you to check out if you need to do reporting. There are walk-throughs for reporting in Windows Forms, Server Side Web Forms, and Client Side Web Forms.

I'm pointing this out just to let you know it is there and that you don't need to reinvent the wheel to do reporting. But there is a ton of information to cover to put a working example in this writing, and it would be no more detailed than the walk-through that you can see online on MSDN.

Exporting Tables to XML

The last topic I want to cover is exporting a table to XML. There are times when you want to take a DataTable that you have and store it in a format to access somewhere else. The easiest way to do that is to store it as XML. There are some things to be aware of before you do this. First, you must have the TableName property of the DataTable set before you attempt to export it. Note that the TableName isn't the name of the table in the database; it is a name that you set. The following code will do the export for you:

```
OleDbDataAdapter dadapter = new OleDbDataAdapter("Select * from Customers",
connstr.ConnectionString);
                        DataTable dt = new DataTable();
                        dadapter.Fill(dt);
                        dt.TableName = "test_table";
                        dt.WriteXml("c:\\users\\michael\\table.xml");
```

This code assumes you are using the code that we used earlier in the chapter where the connstr object is already created. But in any code where you have a DataTable, the last two lines will do the export.

When you do the export of the Customers table in the Northwind database, you will get something that looks like the following:

```
<?xml version="1.0" standalone="true"?>
<DocumentElement>
<test_table>
<ID>1</ID>
<Company>Company A</Company> <Last_x0020_Name>Bedecs</Last_x0020_Name>
<First_x0020_Name>Anna</First_x0020_Name>
<Job_x0020_Title>Owner</Job_x0020_Title>
<Business_x0020_Phone>(123)555-0100</Business_x0020_Phone>
<Fax_x0020_Number>(123)555-0101</Fax_x0020_Number>
<Address>123 1st Street</Address>
<City>Seattle</City>
<State_x002F_Province>WA</State_x002F_Province>
<ZIP_x002F_Postal_x0020_Code>99999</ZIP_x002F_Postal_x0020_Code>
<Country_x002F_Region>USA</Country_x002F_Region>
<Attachments/>
</test_table>
...
</DocumentElement>
```

I want you to notice a couple of things. First, if you have spaces in your field names, the code will replace the space with _x0020_. So, if you are writing something to import into another application, it would be best to not have spaces in your field names. Second, the name you give the table should not have spaces, or they will be replaced similar to the above. Finally, note that this rendering doesn't signify the object type. If you remember back to when you wrote the web service, the object type of `DataTable` was where `DocumentElement` is. So, where in an XML Web Service, you can return the XML for a DataTable and place that right into a DataTable, you can't do that directly with this XML. You will get an error that it cannot infer the data schema. So, to be able to load into a new table, you need to also export the schema and then load it before you load the table. To export the schema, place this line right before you write the XML:

```
dt.WriteXmlSchema("c:\\users\\michael\\tableschema.xml");
```

Then, when you want to read the file into a `DataTable`, you use the following lines:

```
DataTable dt = new DataTable();
dt.ReadXmlSchema("c:\\users\\michael\\tableschema.xml");
dt.ReadXml("c:\\users\\michael\\table.xml");
```

If your user wrote a query and returned data that he wanted to access later, you could let him do this and then you could bind this data to a grid in the future. This is very similar to what you might do in Access for writing an ADO recordset to a file.

Wrap-Up

The main goal in all of this was to give you usable examples of code in C# for working with databases. Hopefully, if you had been working in Classic VB or VBA, you have found this helpful. As I stated earlier, I had the idea to write this when I found some items so difficult with very little in the way of help online. Once I figured it out, it took two or three lines of code to do what I needed. In the past, you could always count on good example code shown in context in help. With C#, there are some good examples, but many either just show the method you are looking up and the different overloads it takes, or the example will be against some static data that they load at runtime. While that is certainly better than nothing, I felt that some better examples with code that is shown in context would get people going. On most of the topics covered, there are so many more details, properties, methods, etc., that you can access. I suggest that you explore those as you go. Once the object is available, you can explore very easily.

One other thing that you may have noticed is that I don't write examples that write to the console. Typically, I create a form and have a text box to take the value or I show it in a `MessageBox`. You could change any of the message boxes to write to the console. For me, I like the break in the action of the program to let me see what is going on. It isn't something that I would have in live code for an application for a client, but for debugging, I find it much easier to do that, even more so than putting in breakpoints in the code.

Good luck with your further exploration of C#.

About the Author

Michael Schmalz works in financial services and performs business and technology consulting in a variety of industries. He has done technical editing for O'Reilly on several Microsoft Office books and authored *Integrating Excel and Access* (O'Reilly). Michael has a degree in Finance from Penn State. He lives with his wife and children in Pennsylvania.

Get even more for your money.

Join the O'Reilly Community, and register the O'Reilly books you own. It's free, and you'll get:

- $4.99 ebook upgrade offer
- 40% upgrade offer on O'Reilly print books
- Membership discounts on books and events
- Free lifetime updates to ebooks and videos
- Multiple ebook formats, DRM FREE
- Participation in the O'Reilly community
- Newsletters
- Account management
- 100% Satisfaction Guarantee

Signing up is easy:

1. **Go to: oreilly.com/go/register**
2. **Create an O'Reilly login.**
3. **Provide your address.**
4. **Register your books.**

Note: English-language books only

To order books online:
oreilly.com/store

For questions about products or an order:
orders@oreilly.com

To sign up to get topic-specific email announcements and/or news about upcoming books, conferences, special offers, and new technologies:
elists@oreilly.com

For technical questions about book content:
booktech@oreilly.com

To submit new book proposals to our editors:
proposals@oreilly.com

O'Reilly books are available in multiple DRM-free ebook formats. For more information:
oreilly.com/ebooks

Spreading the knowledge of innovators   oreilly.com

©2010 O'Reilly Media, Inc. O'Reilly logo is a registered trademark of O'Reilly Media, Inc. 00000

Have it your way.

Milton Keynes UK
Ingram Content Group UK Ltd.
UKHW051914250524
443179UK00008B/410